"It hurts me too
Children's experiences of domestic violence and refuge life

Alex Saunders

with

Carole Epstein and Gill Keep
ChildLine

Thangam Debbonaire
Women's Aid Federation England

Preface by
Jan Pahl
National Insitute for Social Work

1995

This resource is to be returned on
or before the last date below

6/6/03		
13·12·07		
18/9/08		
2/4/09		

CONTENTS

NOTE OF THANKS FROM ALEX SAUNDERS

I would like to thank everyone who has helped in the preparation and writing of this publication, in particular Jenny Clifton and Jo Tulloch. Special thanks must be extended to the four adults who agreed to be interviewed, and whose experiences and opinions have so richly informed this work and to Joanne for sharing her feelings as a married women subjected to male violence and the effect on her children.

I would also like to thank the following people for their help and advice: Maureen O'Hara at the Children's Legal Centre; Rebecca Dobash at the University of Wales; Nickie Charles at the University College of Swansea; Anne Clarke at the University of Leicester; Fiona Buchanan, Scottish Women's Aid, first national children's worker and now working for Southern Women's Community Health Centre in Australia; Gill Keep and Carole Epstein at ChildLine; Thangam Debbonaire at the Women's Aid Federation England; and particular thanks to Jan Pahl at the National Institute for Social Work for her support and commitment to the publication of this research.

Finally I would like to thank Linda for her boundless emotional, practical and intellectual support.

> This work is dedicated to my mum. Her courage in the face of
> appalling circumstances and her commitment to her children
> will be the source of lifelong inspiration.

Additional Contributors

We should like to thank Chrissie Poole most warmly for her hard work and high standards in typing the original manuscript. Our thanks also go to Caroline McKinlay for editing and overseeing the production of this publication.

PREFACE

"If it weren't for refuges there'd be a lot of funerals". This comment, by a young woman who spent fourteen months in a refuge when she was eight years old, may serve to set the scene for this remarkable book, which draws together three different perspectives on its topic.

The original initiative for this book came from Alex Saunders. His contribution is based on personal experience, original research and an up-to-date knowledge of the literature. The interviews with adult survivors provide a vivid account of what a child experiences when his or her mother is systematically abused by her husband, while his knowledge of other work ensures that the interview material is set in a broader context. It is characteristic of Alex that he has not produced his research independently, even though it merits publication in its own right, but that he has welcomed the opportunity to work with colleagues who bring other perspectives to the topic.

The second contribution broadens the picture by drawing on the experience which ChildLine has accumulated from children themselves. Carole Epstein and Gill Keep have analysed the records kept by those who respond to children's telephone calls. Their chapter highlights the pain felt by children who live with domestic violence, the isolation which they experience and the courage with which they try to do something about the situation. The evidence from ChildLine underlines how rarely social workers become involved and how important teachers are in providing help and support to children.

The third contribution comes from Thangam Debbonaire, who is the National Children's Officer for the Women's Aid Federation England. Over the past twenty years Women's Aid has provided shelter for hundreds of thousands of women and children: one of its priorities has always been to recognise and care for the emotional and educational needs of the children who come to the refuges. This chapter shows how often statutory agencies fail to help women and children, or even exacerbate the problems that they face, and underlines how much has been achieved by the refuge movement.

Recommendations for policy and practice are an essential part of a book like this. Article 19 of the United Nations Convention on the Rights of the Child states that children have "the right to protection from all forms of violence, abuse, neglect or exploitation". Reading about the experiences of the children and about the work of front-line services inevitably raises questions about what can be done to protect children, to provide longer term help, or to prevent violence against women and its damaging effects on families. The recommendations range widely, reflecting the wide spread of expertise among the authors of the book, and cover the law, education, health and social services.

At the National Institute for Social Work we are very pleased to be able to co-publish this book. Social workers have a statutory responsibility for the welfare of children. However, in the past they have shown a tendency to take wife abuse less seriously than child abuse. The book shows that violence against women hurts children too, and sets out standards for good practice for those responsible for planning and providing social services. In particular it underlines the importance of refuges in providing support for women and children, and the urgent need for more secure funding for their work, which is both a local and a national responsibility. This authoritative and compelling book should be essential reading for all who are concerned about the welfare of children and families.

Dr Jan Pahl
Director of Research
National Institute for Social Work

PART ONE BY ALEX SAUNDERS

INTRODUCTION

The last two decades have seen violence against women exposed world-wide as a major social issue, but little attention has been paid to the children who witness this violence. Most children who witness violence against their mothers do so in isolation and silence. Children quickly learn that to talk openly about violence is either unacceptable or dangerous. This silence is compounded by a deeply entrenched cultural belief in western society that it is better not to discuss upsetting events with children. The sparse research that has been undertaken has further victimised child witnesses. Professionals disregard some of the complex and diverse coping mechanisms children possess by labelling them as psychosomatic disorders, personality defects or the beginnings of an 'addiction to violence'. Women survivors of male violence are already familiar with these labels.

My motivation to understand this subject stems from my personal experience of growing up against a backdrop of violence perpetrated by my father against my mother. In 1977, at the age of thirteen, I witnessed the final act of physical violence my mother was to receive at the hands of my father. Although I had heard my mother viciously and systematically beaten many times, my father had been careful to exclude myself and my brother from actually witnessing his actions. On this occasion, as my mother entered the room he twice punched down on the back of her head, then he forcibly threw her against the wall. His frenzied attack only ceased when he realised that I and one of my friends sat petrified on the sofa.

My witnessing of that attack proved to be a cathartic event. The 'conspiracy of silence' that had engulfed our family had been broken. The following morning my mother and I left home, and by evening we were preparing ourselves for our first night in a women's refuge. For over eighteen months the refuge provided my mother and me with safe accommodation alongside a sympathetic and supportive environment in which to re-organise our lives.

My mother speaks with a great deal of warmth and affection about the emotional and practical support she received at the refuge. However, my own feelings about this experience are ambiguous. I feel a huge amount of gratitude towards the refuge movement generally, and 'my' refuge in particular, for offering us the chance to escape years of violence, abuse and

1

fear. Yet what should be unqualified praise of the refuge has been tempered by a belief that my own needs during this time were not fully recognised or appreciated.

My most pressing need was to break the years of enforced silence, to speak out, to describe and make sense of my own experience of living with and growing up in an environment of violence directed against my mother. Yet in amongst the myriad of competing personal and practical demands within the refuge this opportunity never arose.

It has not been comfortable for me to confront the question of how the refuge met my needs. In a climate where refuges stand out as one of the few islands of hope for women fighting 'one of the oldest forms of intimate domination' (Dobash and Dobash, 1992, 285), the boundary between constructive debate and undermining the movement has felt particularly blurred. This confusion has been compounded by my gender, as a male questioning a movement that has provided safety and support for thousands of women and their children. Most important of all is an unshakeable feeling that I may in some way be betraying a refuge which gave my mother and myself protection and support when it was needed most.

Despite these inhibitions my study of the experience of children in women's refuges grew out of my personal experience. In other words, I have used my own experience to highlight certain areas and questions which I believe merit explanation.

Part One can be divided into three main themes. Firstly, it is important to gain a much wider understanding of the effects of violence against women upon children. Secondly, there is a need for a greater awareness of the experiences of children in women's refuges and their implications. Finally, the role of social workers with children of abused women must be examined, in particular their overall contribution to the care and support children receive.

To assess the impact upon children of violence against their mothers and the experience of life in a refuge, I interviewed four adults who lived as children in women's refuges. I do not intend to make sweeping claims about the empiricism of the research or the generality of my findings. It is important to set these interviews in context. These adults were children in refuges between 1978 and 1980, so more than fifteen years has elapsed. Refuges and childwork have changed and developed considerably in this time. Nevertheless it is my belief that the dialogue is just as relevant today.

The purpose of the interviews is to give a flavour of the issues that a small sample of adults who lived as children in refuges regard as important. These retrospective accounts provide a channel of communication that links childhood experiences from the past with an adult perspective. Reading such personal accounts may help to stimulate pressure for change and hasten the process of reform in the here and now. This untapped resource can provide valuable insights and should contribute to the future development of services.

Chapter One explores some of the effects upon children of living with violence directed against women. I suggest that if refuge workers and social workers are to work effectively with these children they require considerable knowledge and awareness from the child's perspective of the experience of being a child witness.

Chapter Two attempts to give children a voice by articulating children's experiences and their perceptions of life in a women's refuge. I present extensive material from my interviews. I propose that it is vital to argue for greater awareness of children's rights and welfare within refuges.

The potential for social workers to play a substantially different role with children of abused women than that currently adopted is developed in Chapter Three. Much greater awareness of the issues surrounding violence against women is required if social workers are to help both women and children survive the practical and psychological effects of male violence. I shall highlight how recent developments in the law as well as children's rights can be used to empower both women and children. I conclude by drawing together the philosophical and practical developments which combined could help children in their struggle to overcome the effects of male violence.

CHAPTER ONE

CHILDREN OF ABUSED WOMEN

"I had been in bed for five minutes waiting for my mummy. She was doing her teeth in the bathroom. My dad went into the bathroom. He was saying 'Do you still love me?' He was really cross - very, very cross. The door was closed. I heard a wallop and went into the bathroom. She was being strangled and I pulled him off. His hands were on her neck and he was squeezing. He pushed me out of the room. The door slammed shut and he bolted it. I shouted that I was going to call the police."

Daniel told Cardiff Crown Court his father walked past him on the stairs after getting a knife from the kitchen. "I tried to grab his leg but he just carried on," he said. "I heard her dying screams. I saw the knife in my mum's neck. I tried to give her the kiss of life. Then I looked at her and she was dead. I pulled the knife out slightly but I knew she was dead".

The above statement, reported in Today newspaper, was made by a 10-year old boy as he relived in court the night he witnessed his mother's killing (Today, 11.11.92). This child's recent ordeal is a particularly extreme example of a common experience for many children, that of witnessing prolonged and regular violence in the home.

Child witnesses of violence against women

Many of the difficulties in obtaining accurate information about violence against women also apply to the experience of child witnesses. These problems are exaggerated by the lack of research about children as survivors of violence against women.

Defining a child witness extends beyond establishing the child's direct observation of their father (or other intimate partner of their mother) threatening or hitting their mother. Children may hear this behaviour from another part of the house without actually seeing the violence. They may also be exposed to the results of this violence without witnessing its instigation. For example, children may see the bruises or other injuries clearly visible on their mother; or the emotional consequences of fear, hurt, intimidation or anger may be apparent to them (Jaffe, Wolfe and Wilson,

1990, 17). In addition to this emotional abuse some children are also physically and/or sexually abused as part of the experience of violence against their mothers.

Carlson (1984) claims that 3.3 million children in the USA between the ages of three and seventeen are annually exposed to what they describe as 'parental violence'. Other estimates include figures of 58 per cent (Dobash and Dobash, 1984, 279), 90 per cent (Queensland Domestic Violence Task Force, 1988; hereafter referred to as Task Force), whilst Walker (1979) describes how 87 per cent of abused women claimed that their children knew about the violence. Incredibly the study by Jaffe *et al.* (1990) found that almost all of the children they interviewed were able to offer detailed accounts of violence that their mothers or fathers never realised the children had witnessed. I am sure that Sandra speaks for many children when she says that "*it was part of life. You had it since you were born*" (Sandra 1992, aged 23).

Children's responses to witnessing their mother being assaulted by their father vary according to a multitude of factors, including age, sex, stage of development and role in the family. Other factors such as social class, ethnic origin and the special needs a child may have independent of the violence are also key determinants. In addition, the family "*displays differential power relations between mother and father and also relates differently to male and female children. This is why we must be careful about making bland references to 'parents' and 'children' as these ideas mask the important differences within families*" (Frost and Stein, 1989, 8). Nevertheless it is still possible to make some general comments which are valid.

Whilst some children play an active role in trying to deter the violence, others are immobilised and silenced by terror, confusion and shame. One woman's account of her husband's vicious attack vividly illustrates this point.

... I found myself crumpled up on the floor in great pain and couldn't call for my daughter to help. All I was capable of doing was moaning. My daughter who was eleven years came down and wanted to know what I was doing on the floor, and was eventually about to get me up. She was afraid to stay in the house and went out the back door ... He came into the hall an hour later to hit me, and my daughter saw this and screamed. This stopped

5

him. Her younger brother came running to see what was wrong. They were both clinging to each other, crying. (Pizzey, 1974, 50)

In the Dobash's 1984 study they also discovered that children typically screamed, cried or fled to hide. Some tried to run for help, others tried to pull the assailant from the woman. In almost all cases the response of the children was some form of passive or active support for the woman.

He would go out and get drunk and come back in and beat my mum up with me watching and listening. He would keep it up all night so that my mum would have to get up and go into my little sister's bed, but he would come in and pull her out. When he beat up my mum, my big brother would try to stop him but my dad would push him away so he would call someone like me to help him but my dad would just shout at me to go away and then push me. Regina, aged 13. (Pizzey, 1974, 67)

Yet in the midst of adversity some children find hidden strengths and resources that are invaluable, and sometimes lifesaving. For example, accounts in numerous publications have detailed children of all ages phoning the police for assistance (Hoff, 1990, 205; Jaffe, Wolfe and Wilson, 1990, 52; Task Force, 1988, 102).

Sophia remembers her own experience of assisting her mum with a mixture of horror and pride:

She [Sophia's mum] was doing his tea, but because it wasn't ready there and then when he walked through the door, he got hold of her, dragged her on the floor, took her shoe and he started whacking her on the head with her shoe. He made her head bleed, [so] I grabbed a purse and I whacked it over his back trying to stop him from hitting my mum. He realised what he'd done, so I'd saved my mum's life really because he was going to kill her. I ran out of the house and asked our neighbour to call the police. I was five when I done that. What five year old would think of doing that? (Sophia, aged 21)

Jaffe *et al.* (1990) suggest that girls in particular seek to protect younger siblings during violent episodes and offer support or reassurance in the aftermath of the violent behaviour. A number of women have attributed their eventual escape to the emotional and practical support provided by their children (Hoff, 1990, 205; Task Force, 1988, 102-103).

Links between child abuse and violence against women

There is growing evidence of a link between child abuse and violence against women.

I'll never forget when he hit me the first time. I heard a choking sound coming from the bedroom. I walked in and he had my son by the throat, choking him. He wouldn't let go no matter how I begged and pleaded. I hit him across the face and he threw my son across the room and turned on me. (Task Force, 1988, 103)

Bowker *et al.* (1988) found that men who beat their wives also physically abused their children in 70 per cent of cases. A plethora of studies from America (Walker, 1979), Britain (Gayford, 1975), Australia (Task Force, 1988) and Denmark (Christensen, 1990) feature accounts from women which support this assertion.

According to O'Hara (1992) there is little research as yet concerning the relationship between sexual abuse of children and sexual and physical violence against their mothers. Stark and Flitcraft (1985) report on a sample group of 116 children identified as suspected targets of child sexual abuse. Among the mothers of these children 45 per cent had been abused by their male partner. They argue that wife abuse is the major precipitating context of child abuse and the male abuser is the typical child abuser. In addition,

... the personal accounts of both sexual abuse survivors and women who have experienced domestic violence suggest that many men sexually abuse both adult women and children. One indicator of the links between these forms of abuse is the fact that refuges for battered women were among the first institutions in this country to recognise the prevalence of the sexual abuse of children. (O'Hara, 1992, 4)

However, it is important to acknowledge that there may also be important differences in cause and manifestation between sexual abuse and other forms of child abuse.

Abuse of children even extends to the womb. There are many reports of women who found that instead of pregnancy offering a respite from violence their abuse only increased during this time (Gayford, 1975; Hoff, 1990, 56-

61; Pizzey, 1974, 77-82). Miscarriage resulting from abuse has also been widely reported.

The worst thing he ever did was kill my daughter. I was nearly seven months pregnant when D. bashed me one night. After a week of pain in my back, little A., that's what I named her, was born and only lived three days. She didn't have a chance. The doctors found scars and damage to the placenta, my daughter's only life support while I was carrying her.
(Task Force, 1988, 104)

The effects upon children

In Part Two of this book Epstein and Keep present a first hand account of the effects of violence against women upon children. From calls from children phoning ChildLine about domestic violence, it can be seen that children's responses are often complex and conflicting. Similarly, the personal accounts of children presented in *Breaking Through* (Women's Aid Federation of England, 1989; hereafter referred to as WAFE) offer an accurate and painful abridgement of a range of different reactions. Children feel guilty, confused, angry, powerless, different, bitter and rejected.

I remember fantasising that my parents would die - then felt really guilty - because I wasn't allowed to express my feelings. I didn't realise that it was OK to have bad thoughts.

When you can't express how unhappy you are you learn not to bother - you feel rejected and bitter - it flattens you, it stops you trying.

I wasn't even aware of having any rights.

I used to smile so that people wouldn't know.
This feeling of having skeletons in the cupboard carries on into adulthood.

I used to fantasise about being a 'normal' child.
(WAFE, 1989, 26-27)

The multitude of influences that affect children's *responses* to violence against their mothers are also critical factors influencing the *effects* upon children of this experience. Children sometimes feel guilty if they do not come to the aid of their mother.

I remember being in my bedroom when I was 10 years-old and my friend saying to me 'John, John, your dad's hitting your mum'. But I didn't go down there. I didn't help her. When I had to show courage I didn't have any, so in a very simplistic way I think I seek out situations now where I can be courageous. (John, 1992, aged 27)

Frequently children feel that they are responsible for defusing their father's anger. Guilt is often accompanied by self-blame and the feeling that they have in some way 'caused' their father to be violent.

I think we blamed ourselves for the violence because he used to hit her [mum] if he didn't have money for drink, but we were eating the money coz it was for food. (Sandra, 1992, aged 23)

Louise [a young girl of only a few years] ... said that she knew why she had come to the shelter. Louise claimed that she kept leaving her tricycle on the front walk, contrary to her father's repeated instruction. 'One day I got him so mad that he hit mom.' Louise was sure that she was to blame for the violence. (Jaffe, Wolfe and Wilson, 1990, 2)

Confusing feelings about blame appear in comments from children of all ages. Children have expressed feelings of anger directed against their mother for not protecting herself or the children, as well as blaming her for causing the violence. At the same time children still express love for their mothers. Other children want to be with their fathers although they want the violence to end. Some children are so concerned with their mothers' distress that they keep private their own grief.

From the above personal descriptions it is evident that children can be left with a great many painful memories and conflicting emotions, some of which do not recede with time.

If I saw it [her father hitting her mum] now I'd just take a knife and stab him. (Clara, 1992, aged 19)

I can remember when my dad used to beat my mum up right back to when I was five. He used to beat her up really badly in front of me. I can remember that far back and I still can't get it out my head now; I still can't get it out my head. (Sophia, 1992, aged 21)

*The memories of the violence torment you. When I heard that he [Sandra's dad] was dying I thought that I ought to see him. But then I remembered what he'd done. I felt like I was betraying mum even by **thinking** about going to see him.* (Sandra, 1992, aged 23)

Based on studies of child development in what Jaffe *et al.* (1990) call 'normal' families, a range of adjustment difficulties can be identified. Difficulties include: increased levels of anxiety for both males and females (Forsstrom-Cohn and Rosenbaum, 1985); psychosomatic illnesses, including headaches, abdominal complaints, asthma, peptic ulcers, rheumatoid arthritis, stuttering and enuresis (Alessi and Hearn, 1984); depression (Forsstrom-Cohn and Rosenbaum, 1985); sadness, withdrawal and fear (Jaffe, Wolfe and Wilson, 1990, 37); lower rating in social competence, particularly for boys (Wolfe, Jaffe, Wilson and Zak, 1985); a reduction in understanding social situations including thoughts and feelings of people involved (Rosenberg, 1984).

More observable behaviours have been identified, such as: excessive cruelty to animals, teenage boys beating their girlfriends (Task Force, 1988); disobedience, destructiveness in younger boys (Wolfe, Jaffe, Wilson and Zak, 1985); nervous, withdrawn and anxious demeanour in younger girls (Hughes, 1986); more difficult temperaments and more aggressive behaviour in both sexes (Holden and Ritchie, 1991, 311); children running away from home (Jaffe, Wolfe and Wilson, 1990, 28-29).

This body of research provides important insights into the effects of violence against women upon their children. Unfortunately this work has invariably occurred within the rigid and ethnocentric framework of children's cognitive development stages depicted in most psychological theory (Freeman, 1983, 210). As Hoyles argues, "... *the child-study industry has based its research largely on psychology which concentrates on the child as an individual, is usually ethnocentric, and ignores the political context of childhood"* (Hoyles, 1989, 32).

Research of a similar kind, derived in large part from social learning theory, claims an intergenerational transmission of violence. Advocates of this approach suggest that violence against women is learned behaviour, following a pattern copied from childhood in a violent home and leading to cycles of violence in subsequent generations.

This is not only taken to mean that the man learns to be violent because of a violent childhood, but that the woman also learns from her childhood to tolerate violence, to provoke it, or - most offensive of all - to grow to need it. (WAFE, 1989, 55)

This idea developed from work which had sought explanations of male violence in women's behaviour, and it gained prominence as a means of explaining why women stay in violent relationships (see for example, Gayford, 1975; Pizzey, 1974; Pizzey and Shapiro, 1982). According to Jaffe *et al.* (1990) the cycle of violence concept is attractive largely because it accounts for the higher rates of violent behaviour often described among children from violent families.

However, the quality of the evidence is far from convincing. Re-evaluating the data supplied by Straus *et al.* (1980), Stark and Flitcraft suggest that 90 per cent of the men from 'violent' homes as children and 80 per cent of the men from the 'most violent' homes are not currently abusing (Stark and Flitcraft, 1985, 157). As Dobash and Dobash maintain,

Children may learn to accept, admire, emulate, or expect such behaviour, but they may also be repulsed by it and reject its use. It would be naive in the extreme to assume that a child is such a simple creature that he or she learns only one thing from what he or she observes, and that is to emulate the observed behaviour in a robot fashion ...
(Dobash and Dobash, 1979, 153)

A highly significant point not to be overlooked is the fear this theory can strike in the minds of those who come from violent backgrounds.

After I had my son I became obsessed with my violent background. I just had to know about my dad. I was convinced that because he had been violent I would also be violent to my son. It's a terrible burden to have to live with, and which despite everything you know to be true never quite seems to go away. (John)

The 'inevitability' of a violent future is described by John as one of the most disabling and paralysing feelings he has experienced. Rutter and Madge's

11

work on 'cycles of disadvantage' is particularly relevant here. They suggest that unfortunately research has concentrated for the most part on what goes wrong in children's development. Little attention has been paid to the factors which enable people to overcome an unpromising start to life or to take later stresses in their stride. They repeatedly emphasise that children raised in the most deplorable circumstances develop into what they describe as 'normal' children (Rutter and Madge, 1976, 325). The key point is that we need to examine the factors which mediate the bad experiences of childhood and facilitate a break with the 'cycles of disadvantage'.

The issue here is not whether or not women [or children] are affected by their experience of violence, clearly anyone would be but we must consider the implications and limitations of the way we conceive of their predicament. (Dobash and Dobash, 1992, 224)

Discussing social learning and child development theories provides a base for considering how the impact of violence can be mediated in later years by positive relationships and experiences which build self-esteem and challenge stereotypical male and female behaviour. The central concern for social workers and refuge workers is to consider the factors which either reinforce or ameliorate the effects of an abusive or deprived childhood.

Children's coping mechanisms

Whilst childhood has become *"the most analysed and overstaged life phase in our developmental cycle"* (Suransky, 1982, 21), paradoxically this 'view from above' has ignored how children themselves, as active participants, perceive and define their world and personal struggles.

Children are engaged in constant struggles to comprehend the violence and their predicament. Bass and Davis' (1992) powerful volume for women survivors of child sexual abuse offers valuable insights that are equally relevant for child witnesses of violence against women.

There is a continuum of coping behaviours. You may have run away from home or turned to alcohol or drugs. You may have become a super-achiever, excelling in school and taking care of your brothers and sisters at home. You may have forgotten what happened to you, withdrawn into yourself, or cut off your feelings. With few resources for taking care of yourself, you survived with whatever means were available. Many survivors criticize themselves for the ways they coped. You may not want to admit some of the things you had to do to survive. But coping is nothing to be ashamed of. You survived, and its important to honor your resourcefulness. (Bass and Davis, 1992, 40)

Some of these coping techniques described above may have developed over time into strengths, for example being self sufficient, developing a sense of humour, being good in a crisis. Others may be less positive, such as stealing, aggression, addiction and isolation.

In conjunction with each child's own interpretation of the violence and coping mechanisms are other potentially ameliorating factors that may account for a child's resilience. Garmezy (1983) found that support within the family system and support from outside it were critical protective factors. Bass and Davis discuss how the impact of child sexual abuse is affected by the response of others.

The way the abuse was handled when you were a child has a lot to do with its subsequent impact. If a child's disclosure is met with compassion and effective intervention, the healing begins immediately. But if no one noticed or responded to your pain, or if you were blamed, not believed, or suffered further trauma, the damage was compounded. (Bass and Davis, 1992, 34)

For many women the process of dealing with the effects of male violence begins with their experience in a women's refuge. The vital support work which helps women to rebuild their lives is also required for children arriving at the refuge. This is evident from the testament in this chapter and is illustrated by refuge workers' descriptions of the sorts of problems that are encountered amongst the children.

CHAPTER TWO

CHILDREN IN WOMEN'S REFUGES

Listening to the truth of someone's life is a privilege and an honor.
(Bass and Davis, 1992, 100)

When a woman seeks refuge from violence her children face equal crisis and disruption in their lives. Whilst violence against women is often trivialised or ignored in wider society, the children involved are in an even more vulnerable position, having no independent voice. Although they represent over two-thirds of the refuge population, in such a hectic and often emotionally fraught environment children continue to remain relatively invisible. This is particularly worrying given that over 15,000 children of every age pass through WAFE refuges (Ball, 1990) and over 2,000 through Welsh Women's Aid refuges each year (Charles, 1991).

This does not mean that the refuge movement has been unconcerned with children's rights and welfare. From the very outset refuges in this country have been aware of the practical and emotional needs of children entering refuges. In North America shelter staff have documented the trauma experienced by child witnesses, and this material has played a significant role in highlighting the need for more intensive community interventions. Elsewhere, for example in Denmark, work with children of abused women is already more developed and better resourced than in the UK (O'Hara, 1992, 5; Hester and Radford, 1992).

Women's Aid has to cope with a wide range of children from babies to adolescents, all from a wide variety of cultural and social backgrounds. Similarly the ages of children in the refuge from one week to the next may vary considerably. Two studies, conducted 10 years apart, showed that over 80 per cent of children were below secondary school age. The numbers of pre-school and primary age children tended to be roughly equal. Although the number of teenagers in refuges at the time of the two studies was comparatively small, they still constituted between 10 per cent and 20 per cent of the refuge population.

Some children move in and out of refuges at very short notice, whilst others can stay for up to two years awaiting rehousing (McKinlay and Singh, 1991, 5). Ball (1990) found that whilst up to 27 per cent of children only stayed for a week, 36 per cent were in a refuge for six months or more. Charles asserts that within refuges a trend towards longer periods of residence from women and children is developing, often in accommodation which is not designed for this purpose (Charles, 1991, 10).

While refuges continue to lack adequate resources to provide the level of care and support required by the women, children in refuges will be particularly impoverished. Moreover, it is evident that the voices of children involved remain largely unheard. Whilst individual comments and indirect references have been documented in some Women's Aid publications (see for example, Binney, Harkell and Nixon, 1981; SWA, n.d.; WAFE, n.d.; 1989), there remains a need to conduct comprehensive research and to record and consider the perceptions and views of children who have experienced life in a refuge.

The specific experience of children from ethnic minority backgrounds remains relatively unknown. Of the nine refuges given grants as part of a recent joint project between the National Council of Voluntary Child Care Organisations (NCVCCO) and WAFE, three catered specifically for women from minority groups; two for Asian women, one for Latin American women (Ball, 1990). Regrettably in her evaluation of this project Ball does not specify the cultural background of people quoted in the report. In a similar vein the first comprehensive study to look specifically at black women's experience of male violence in the home (Mama, 1989), including refuge provision, makes very few references to the experiences of their children.

The dearth of research concerning children's experience of refuge life means that their position of relative powerlessness and isolation within refuges is reinforced. The four year-old report by Ball (1990) on the nine jointly funded refuges in England represents one of the few documents which specifically highlights children's issues and children's workers in refuges. As a result I have made full use of this document. However, it should be noted that Ball's survey covered a very small sample of refuges in England, and therefore comprehensive conclusions should not be drawn from this material. In addition all the children's worker posts created as part of this project were part-time, in the main 20 hours per week, with only one or two being longer.

In recent years an increasing body of material has begun to emerge. For example, the production by WAFE of a series of children's issues briefing papers, and discussion at two major conferences and several smaller conferences during the last eighteen months concerning children and 'domestic violence'. Debonnaire's chapter in Part Two of this book offers up-to-date information about children in refuges. The rest of this chapter is primarily devoted to those with personal experience of refuge life between 1978 and 1980 to share.

Arrival

Both Clara and Sophia vividly remember how it all began.

I remember leaving home. Mum and me walking down the road with a pram full of my toys ... (Clara, 1992, aged 19; in refuge during 1979, aged 5 on arrival)

I remember my mum saying to me that we were going up the launderette. She had two bags full of clothes and she kept saying that we were going to do the washing. But we ended up at this strange house that was a right state. (Sophia, 1992, aged 21; in refuge between 1979-80, aged 8 on arrival)

It was scary. Frightening. Coming away from your home and going into this strange place, not knowing anyone. Different people, different place, different kids. I got very disturbed. I played up. In fact, I was a right little sod, so was Simon [Sophia's brother], but I reckon that was us reacting to what we'd been through. I think the kids suffer more because they don't understand these disturbing things. They know there is something wrong but they don't know what it is do they? (Sophia, 1992, aged 21; in refuge between 1979-80; aged 8 on arrival)

A child's view of refuge life

There are a great many advantages and disadvantages about refuge life, which clearly vary from child to child. The following moving account by a young girl nicely captures the anxiety, relief and pleasure of refuge life.

I am ten years of age I came to the refuge on February 16th 1981. When I walked in I didn't think I'd like it so I stayed with my little brother who is now 22 mths old but when I started school I enjoyed it and had lots of friends. The first night I slept in a bunk bed and couldn't sleep I was nervous I don't know why by the next morning I was ok it was warm and comforting not like my own home that was cold because my step father wouldn't let us have the fire on or the electric on so we sat there freezing cold.

The next day the workers came in and spoke to my mum nicely and they were very nice, and my mum said how nice the women were when she came in and how they gave her a cup of coffee and a fag and me and my brother milk and food and I and my mum was pleased. Then she told them about the cab how they went half for paying because she didn't have enough money to pay, and when I got there a little girl named paulette spoke to me then my first friend who came the next night. In the summer holidays they took us out every day and payed for us to go to butlins for a week, and we have an adventure play ground in our garden which they made while we were at butlins. I like the workers very much. And I must thank them for all they have done while I have been at the Refuge. Lynette, London South, (WAFE, n.d., 37-38)

Many children simply feel relieved to have left a violent situation and glad that their mother is similarly free from abuse. *"If it weren't for refuges there'd be a lot of funerals"* (Sophia). The company of other children can also be invaluable, since isolation is a common state for both women and children experiencing male violence. In fact, the communality of experience that is at the corner-stone of refuge empowerment sometimes extends to the children.

I remember some of the kids used to call my nan "nan"! I couldn't understand why they called her nan when she was my nan. In fact, we all seemed to have two or three nans. It was like a big family. You could share other people. (Clara, 1992, aged 19; in refuge during 1979, aged 5 on arrival)

There are also many disadvantages to refuge life. Children will have been uprooted from family and friends, moved away from familiar surroundings including toys, pets, clothes and separated from a father they may love. Children may be too young to understand what is happening or resent the

17

disruption in their lives (McKinlay and Singh, 1991, 5). For some children the benefits of leaving a violent home may not be immediately obvious. Not only is there uncertainty about what will happen next, but the immediate conditions of overcrowding, a lack of privacy and shared rooms add to the pressures.

Arrival at a refuge can bring great relief to children who have been frightened and who may have been abused. However, on some occasions the move itself involves children in new, threatening situations. In the 10-month period of the Ball evaluation she refers to seven instances of men attacking or besieging refuges. Such attacks affect everybody in the refuge and in these circumstances restricted movement outside the refuge may be imposed on children out of fear of violence or abduction (Ball, 1990, 9). Sophia described a particularly terrifying experience that we had both endured at our Essex refuge:

Do you remember that night he [Sophia's dad] came looking for us? When he drove his Jag [Jaguar car] through the refuge door? That was very scary and frightening - everyone hiding under beds and tables. He was screaming out 'if I can't have my kids, I'll kill them'. (Sophia, 1992, aged 21; in refuge between 1979-80, aged 8 on arrival)

Facilities

Binney *et al.*'s (1981) early study of refuges showed a general lack of children's facilities, the consequences of which are summed up by Sandra who was living in a refuge during that period.

There was a concrete garden outside. You felt all walled-up - twelve foot-high it was. It should've been a bit more pleasant for the kids. Outside stuff, like a sandpit. And its not only to make it pleasant. I'm a nursery nurse now and I understand how children learn through play. Things like water, and so on can be very therapeutic. I know it's all money but we didn't have anything like that. (Sandra, 1992, aged 23; in refuge between 1978-79, aged 9 on arrival)

Charles' 1991 study of Welsh Women's Aid refuges makes similarly depressing reading. Of 27 refuges whose facilities were listed 17 had no playroom, although most refuges without a playroom had an outside play

18

area. Where the playroom did not also serve as the women's sitting room, emergency accommodation, storage space or a throughway to other parts of the building, it was often locked to prevent the destruction of toys during unsupervised play. Only six of the refuges were able to offer older children the option of using a quiet room for privacy and retreat, and in most cases this room was being used for the same purpose by women (Charles, 1991, 24). Ball's 1990 study of nine refuges makes a similar point about the lack of space and facilities for older children.

However, more recent information offers evidence of a dramatic improvement in facilities over the last few years. From the most recent annual survey of refuges in England very few refuges are now without a playroom and many have more than one. Funding from charities such as the BBC's Children In Need during the last 2/3 years has enabled over 50 per cent of refuges in England to provide play areas both inside and outdoors, and to purchase equipment, minibuses, toys and so forth. Debonnaire provides further information in Part Two of this book.

Reactions of others

The social stigma often attached to abused women extends to their children (WAFE, n.d., 30). Sandra's story illustrates this point.

I feel so angry at the way everyone was treated. People used to cross the road sometimes ... I remember being treated like a thief in the local sweet shop near the refuge. The shop owner would be watching you to see if you nicked anything just because you lived in a battered wives home. When we bought penny sweets in his shop other kids would just say to him, 'I've got 20 pence worth'. But with me it was 'one, two, three ...', he would count them all out in front of all my friends - silly things like that. It makes you so **angry**. (Sandra, 1992, aged 23; in refuge between 1978-79, aged 9 on arrival)

Most children are not able to talk to friends about being in the refuge and don't tell anyone (Binney, Harkell and Nixon, 1981; WAFE, n.d.).
I never told anyone. I closed up completely. I never used to tell any of my friends what I was going through. (Sophia, 1992, aged 21; in refuge between 1979-8, aged 8 on arrival)

I remember a friend of mine phoned my dad to speak to me, so my dad gave him the phone number of the refuge! This caused quite a stir, but all I was worried about was that this friend might know where I was. I told him that I was at a friend's house who had a lot of noisy kids. (John, 1992, aged 27; in refuge between 1978-80, aged 13 on arrival)

I think a lot about the Refuge but I cannot talk to friends and don't think I will ever want to. Peter - London North East (WAFE, n.d., 38)

When Sandra overcame her reticence and confided in her friend she was particularly bitter at her friend's parents' response.

*They don't wanna know you. They think you're some kind of scum. They look down their noses at you. When I used to walk in the front door of my friend's house they used to say, 'Oh, they live in **there**'.* (Sandra)

Feelings of pain and isolation can be heightened by a lack of awareness by others of the practicalities of life in a refuge.

People's idea of the refuge was dirty kids. Scruffy kids running around with dirty knees, dirty hands, scruffy hair and holes in their clothes. But it wasn't like that at all. (Sandra)

Clara recounted the following story with a potent mixture of anger and amusement.

When I talked to my friends about the refuge they always said 'Oh you poor thing'. It's like they thought we had all been chucked in this one room with a bucket for a toilet! And the things that kids at school used to think we did in there. They thought we were told when to eat dinner, forced to do the washing-up, not allowed to play. Someone thought we had one pair of shoes passed between the whole set of kids. They used to think that if there wasn't enough room in the refuge people used to sleep in tents in the garden! (Clara)

School

Where schools did know of a child's situation there were often reports of teasing. Some children may have to change schools whilst older children may be forced to travel long distances to remain at their existing school, due to the location of the refuge (WAFE, n.d., 30). All of my research participants recalled negative responses from head teachers at a time when they were most in need of support.

I remember my mum kept me from school because she couldn't afford to buy me any shoes. The headmaster sent us £30 to buy some but as soon as I returned to school he kept me in detention for a month. (John)

My dad used to come down to the school to try to see me. I would have to hide until he went away. That's why my headmistress didn't like me. She wanted the perfect school with the perfect mum, perfect dad, 2.2 children and a nice house. So she picked on me instead. The headmistress was always making comments like 'hasn't your mother cut your hair?' or 'can't you afford to go to the hairdressers?'. And it seemed like she was always looking at my uniform for a fault or a crease, 'couldn't mummy iron your uniform?'. Nothing heavy, just subtle digs at me. When I think of what my headmistress put me through when I was in the refuge. I think that's why I went into working with kids. (Sandra)

Father

It is important to recognise the potential loss a child may be experiencing through enforced separation from their father. For some children overcoming the struggle between missing or wanting to see their father whilst simultaneously feeling a sense of guilt and betrayal over these emotions is one of the hardest tasks they ever face. The issue is made more complex by the possibility that the father may have been abusing the child, or by the subsequent anguish continued access may cause the mother.

I wanted a dad. I used to see my friends with a mum and dad and I used to dream about them. But I don't even know him, not really. I have no respect for him. (Sophia)

I really wanted to tell someone that I missed having a dad. Not the one that beat up my mum, but just having a dad. But I didn't feel able to. There were women all around me who were beaten up, bruised, scared and angry at what men had done to them. I felt that I couldn't say anything. (John)

21

Access arrangements are examined in more detail in the following chapter. Despite the intensity of emotions unleashed by these dilemmas none of my research participants were denied access to their father by either their mother, the refuge or social services. In fact the biggest problem was their fathers' not keeping appointments. *"We would get all excited, all dressed up, wait on the corner of the road and he wouldn't show up. I used to hate him for that"* (Sophia).

Mother

For some women the strain of constant abuse means that they do not have the energy or resources to meet their children's needs (NCVCCO, n.d., 4; Task Force, 1988, 110). Not only are women coping with their own emotional needs they are also having to make arrangements for the future.

My mum doesn't have time for me anymore.

It's boring, all the mums sit round and talk about what happened. (SWA, n.d., 6)

I couldn't really talk to my mum about any of it because she had worries of her own. In fact I spent most of my time trying to stop her from drinking too much or talking her out of suicide. (John)

However, this was not always the case.

Any men that used to come and have a dig - and there used to be quite a few that would knock on the door - my mum tended to keep us away from it. And she didn't let us see any of the rows or the fighting going on. I think she thought that we'd had enough of that. (Clara)

In the Ball evaluation several mothers commented on how difficult it was to meet their children's needs immediately after taking refuge.

In the refuge it's the first time you talk to women who have been through what you've been through. You need that time to yourself.

You need a break, the drama of leaving is over...

The kids handled it quite well, but they miss their house and friends. I wonder if I've done the right thing, uprooting them. The boy has gone a bit wild, and his school work has gone down, but I feel depressed and too tired to encourage him. (Ball, 1990, 8)

Children's support workers

The commitment to improving children's experience of refuge life is most clearly expressed by the employment of children's workers. Each Federation employs national workers whose brief is to promote the interests of children in refuges. There is widespread recognition that specialist children's work should be developed within Women's Aid refuges (Ball, 1990; Charles, 1991, 82; McKinlay and Singh, 1991, 5; O'Hara, 1992).

A children's worker is expected to provide educational and recreational activities for the children, to provide appropriate support to meet their emotional and psychological needs, to fundraise for the children, to liaise with local schools, health and social services and to provide some security and continuity for children at a time when their mothers are unlikely to be able to give them all the attention they need.

In recent years WAFE has been campaigning to raise awareness of the crucial role played by children's workers in helping children come to terms with their experiences (McKinlay and Singh, 1991, 5). For some children their mother is the only person they trust, although this often adds further stress to a person who already has a great many unfulfilled needs of her own. Often children's workers are able to act as facilitators in this process, involving joint co-operation and negotiation between the mother, her children and the children's worker. This kind of work builds upon a tradition of feminist oriented practice in the field of child sexual abuse. Programmes concentrate on the restoration of the mother-child relationship, recognising the extreme pressure the mother is under and ending once they are able to protect themselves (Parton, 1990(ii), 58).

Conversely, many children are able to talk to children's workers about past experiences which they have not been able to express to their mothers. For these children they are able to build up a relationship with someone they could trust and who was not personally involved with their particular situation (NCVCCO, n.d., 4). The nine part-time children's workers

23

discussed in Ball's study were all well received by the children themselves. Workers were greeted with warmth and enthusiasm, and the observed play sessions were generally calm and creative.

The response from my research participants towards the children's workers they met fifteen or so years ago was mixed. There was general agreement that the children's workers they met were warm and caring, and that most children enjoyed their company and the activities they organised. Sandra thought they were *"absolutely fantastic, they made you feel really special"* whilst Sophia remembers with real joy *"the way we used to have cocoa in the room before we went to bed, and then she [the children's worker] would read us stories"* (Sophia).

However, there was less praise for the children's workers' ability to spend time exploring children's feelings in the aftermath of arrival.

They didn't ask me anything about what happened to me. They didn't sit down and talk with the children about it, they were more interested in the adults. Sometimes it was simply 'get to bed', go and play somewhere'; it felt like they were saying, 'Get out of the way and let the adults get on with it'. (Sophia)

Everyone at the refuge thought I was so helpful. I was always helping out with the younger kids in the playroom, supporting my mum whenever she was crying, depressed or had got drunk to forget it all. But no-one seemed to have any time for me. So one day I tried to punch a hole in the wall so that someone would pay me some attention. (John)

All of the nine part-time children's workers in the Ball evaluation regretted the limited time they had available to listen to children alone, especially older children. One writes:

I feel very frustrated in the job. The more I do, the more I see how much needs to be done ... I had a long talk with an 8-year old today. He has been here for two months and this is the first opportunity I have had to spend time with him on my own. This boy has lived in absolute terror in his own home. I thought by now I was unshockable, but he has taught me different. He has started to soil himself and show disturbing behaviour, and when we started to talk the floodgates just opened. After three-quarters of an hour I had to go to a meeting. He said, 'I have got so much to say and you haven't got time'. (Ball, 1991, 14)

This frustration was sometimes compounded by the attitudes of general refuge workers. Although refuge workers expressed support for the childcare work, some children's workers did not feel this was supported in practice. Refuge workers were candid about their tendency to forget the needs of children. Consequently many children's workers described their work as having a low status in refuges while they themselves often felt isolated (Ball, 1990, 14).

In order to act as children's advocates in the refuge some workers have established regular children's meetings when children raise and discuss issues in the refuge that are important to them. Where possible these meetings were run by the children themselves (Charles, 1991, 39), and recommendations were taken forward to the general house meetings of the refuge (Ball, 1990, 14).

Some children's workers in the Ball evaluation commented that matters of importance to children were placed as the last item on the agenda at house meetings. In one refuge mothers were unhappy about the idea of a children's meeting, feeling that 'it stirred up trouble'. However, this was not the case in all refuges and the general impression of children's workers was that this and similar initiatives raised the collective consciousness of children's needs in the refuges.

The belief of one woman that children's meetings stir up trouble highlights the tension and difficulties in balancing rights within refuges. This is more clearly expressed through children's workers' handling of acts of violence directed against children as disciplinary action by a parent.

Whilst shelter staff may view empowerment as offering women the skills to parent children in less punitive ways, some women react angrily when they see workers trying to change them or the way they parent their children (Schechter, 1982, 91). Since violence against children is firmly established as an acceptable and necessary form of control in western culture and history (Franklin, 1986; Freeman, 1983; Frost and Stein, 1989; Violence against Children Study Group, 1990), this can create value conflicts and increase stress at a time when women are already under extreme pressure (Hoff, 1990, 203).

25

According to Hoff these factors have resulted in policy being offered in the form of positive role modelling of alternative parent-child interaction rather than direct opposition to physical punishment (Hoff, 1990, 203). Whilst this is a clear recognition of the need to work with parents in order to 'protect' children, seemingly absent in much of this debate is the notion of the right of children not to be abused.

I have discussed the role of children's workers at length because of their critical importance for children. The level of care and support offered to children depends to a large extent on the availability of children's workers. Positive and supportive relationships between children, their mothers and children's support workers can all serve to mediate the effects of the child's experiences.

In the USA the growing recognition of the needs of these children, coupled with greater public awareness and funding, has resulted in many shelters developing specialist services for children (Grusznski, Brink and Edleson, 1988; Jaffe, Wolfe and Wilson, 1990, 95-100; Schechter, 1982, 88-90). They confirm the need for a therapeutic response and some important insights into the needs of child witnesses are gleaned from this work. In particular: the value of granting explicit permission to discuss the violence; eliciting and clarifying the child's perceptions of the violent event; examining the child's position as a witness (for example what the child thought might happen and what should be done); an explanation of the child's blamelessness; a discussion of how further recurrences will be prevented (Silvern and Kaersvang, 1989, 428).

Jaffe, Wolfe and Wilson give useful pointers about the kinds of issues to which refuge/shelter staff should remain sensitive. These include: understanding the child's shock, confusion, anxiety and distress that may exist as a result of witnessing violence against their mothers; being aware of the child's possible ambivalence about his or her relationship with both parents; understanding the child's insecurity about his or her future as well as possible guilt about causing the violence or not being able to prevent it; helping the child to develop a sense of trust and security in the present environment; assisting the child to deal with any distress in moving from familiar surroundings, friends and so forth (Jaffe, Wolfe and Wilson, 1990, 97-98).

26

In Britain the response to child witnesses has taken longer to develop. A key reason is that it has been less resourced than in the USA. The particular needs and experiences of children have always been a concern of staff but until very recently there has been little or no funding for specialist posts.

In the past few years, however, the situation has changed dramatically and a majority of Women's Aid refuges now employ at least one part-time children's support worker. The creation of these posts has led to an increased articulation of children's needs and rights, drawing on the knowledge and awareness gained in the previous twenty years and building on that foundation. WAFE are now committed to a detailed policy on children's rights and are promoting alternatives to physical punishment. More information about current provision and future directions can be found in Debonnaire's chapter in Part Two of this book. Despite these advances, Women's Aid work with children is still often undervalued by funders and consequently under resourced, which continues to place limits on the scope of the work.

Follow up support

When children leave a refuge there is little chance of follow up support. This is an especially important time for children, who may not have the maturity or financial resources to keep in contact with other children from the refuge. Women are strongly encouraged to remain active within the refuge if they wish, and they are seen as an invaluable source of support and inspiration to other women still resident in the refuge. Unfortunately cultivation of this mutually supportive relationship has not been extended to children.

When I went in the refuge I was ashamed. I thought that I wasn't normal, that I was a bad kid and a failure. Maybe if I'd seen kids who had been in the refuge and turned out alright I wouldn't have hated myself so much. (John)

In retrospect

At the end of the interviews I asked each person to voice one thought about their experiences that they would most like others to consider. Both Sandra and John wished to place their reflections within the larger framework of violence against women.

I think there's too much of it [violence against women and children] and its all behind closed doors. We are in [name omitted] and it couldn't be more snooty. When our neighbour found out where we used to live it was 'Oh, how disgusting', and yet she's beaten up next door. (Sandra)

*All the time I was living in a refuge it felt very much like **us and them**. The outside world didn't understand and so I felt very ashamed and isolated. But now I feel quite proud of it really, and in a funny sort of way I actually enjoy thinking that other people will never understand what I went through. It makes me feel strong and special. But in another way I hate that feeling, because it shouldn't been like that - its going on everywhere [violence against women and children] and it should be brought out into the open.* (John)

The children should have their own personal counsellor. Well, not exactly a 'counsellor', I don't like that word, but a sort of big brother or big sister or mate who knows what they are going through and can help them. (Clara)

You get through it by yourself, but it would be nice to have a bit of help because its hard work on your own. (Sophia)

CHAPTER THREE

SOCIAL WORK WITH CHILDREN OF ABUSED WOMEN

Mum used to get very tense before the social worker came, and it put us all on edge. She [the social worker] would come and talk to me but I didn't tell her anything. I'd just been taken away from my dad. I was frightened that if I told her I was upset about all that had happened to me that she would take me away from my mum. So I kept quiet. (Sophia)

There can be very little doubt that social work practice has traditionally been unhelpful to abused women. There is a long and ignominious history of intervention in this field. *"What emerges from all the studies is a concern on the part of social workers to keep families together, to stress the need for reconciliation and to put the interests of children first"* (Smith, 1989, 75). The emphasis on reconciliation leads social workers to marginalise and trivialise the violence experienced by women seeking their assistance (Maynard, 1985, 131-136).

It shouldn't be about reconciliation. All my mum's social worker kept saying to her was 'if you get back together you can be one big happy family'. That's why I want to be a social worker. Even if someone phones me up at 3 'o' clock in the morning and they've got their husband banging on the door I'm straight in the car and I'm round, because I know what its like. (Sandra)

Maynard asserts that social workers modified their indifference to abused women only when they considered the welfare of children to be jeopardised. In these situations social workers' statutory responsibility for children often led to intervention which was in marked contrast to their desire to do nothing that might threaten the survival of a particular family unit. Social worker's concern that children may be at risk because the father is violent has often led them to remove or threaten to remove children from abused mothers (Mama, 1989, 97). This common failure by social workers to distinguish between the abusing and non-abusing parent is particularly disturbing, and the consequences of this approach are often felt by black women and working-class women.

The following woman's experience provides a salient commentary on how this happens, and how the horror of the experience is further compounded for women of a different ethnic origin by racist immigration laws.

Lily Ching's ... young son was temporarily fostered when Lily had returned home from hospital too severely injured to look after him. In her exhausted and powerless state, she felt some anxiety when she was asked to sign papers that she had not found the energy to read. Subsequently she was cautioned by social services that if she remained in the violent situation, so jeopardising her son's safety, they may be forced to remove him from her custody. Once she left, she had to face the even more coercive threat of deportation. (Mama, 1989, 97)

Not surprisingly many women have good reasons for not welcoming social work intervention. Maynard suggests that,

It is not that particular social workers necessarily have malicious attitudes towards battered women, but rather that social work's professional self-image, its training programmes and its definitional duties as laid down by the state, preclude the likelihood of being sympathetically active in dealing with wife beating. (Maynard, 1985, 137)

At the heart of good practice must be an informed knowledge of the issues and effects of violence against women upon both women and children. Furthermore, an approach which also acknowledges the power and gender imbalances within families is likely to result in a very different practice response from that described by Mama (1989) in the case of Lily Ching.

However, attempts to de-individualize child abuse face limitations and contradictions ... Professionals who are directly responsible for a child's welfare have little room or time to take such risks; nor does the woman, who is under pressure to prove she is a good mother. (Parton, 1990 (ii), 49-50).

These dilemmas are not easily resolved. In spite of this it is possible for social workers to pursue policy and practice changes that seek to empower women and children abused by male violence. The impact upon child witnesses of violence against women converges with child protection issues, but in a much broader sense than is currently recognised. Highlighting violence against women as an issue of central concern for social work is the first step to improving the lives of child witnesses. As O'Hara maintains, *"children's welfare cannot in practice be separated from the question of the safety of their primary carers, and this needs to be adequately taken into account when making decisions ..."* (O'Hara, 1992, 5).

Empowering abused women to protect their children

Recognition of the potential links between child abuse and violence against women is crucial to the development of good practice in a number of related areas (O'Hara, 1992, 4). Summarising research into links between child abuse and violence against women Stark and Flitcraft warn that,

These findings have important implications for policy. The authors point out that those who are concerned about child abuse would do well to look towards advocacy and protection of battered mothers as the best means to prevent current child abuse as well as child abuse in the future. (Stark and Flitcraft, 1985, 147)

Failure to take these links seriously can have fatal consequences. The report into the death of Sukina Hammond at the hands of her father suggested that whilst social services were aware of violence against Sukina's mother, they underestimated the threat this posed to Sukina and her sister (O'Hara, 1992, 4). Sukina was removed from the at risk register shortly after a vicious attack upon her mother. *"The likelihood is that the existence of domestic violence appeared to be perceived as acceptable without seeking clarification of the details of the assaults"* (Bridge Child Care Consultancy Service, 1991, 86).

The report criticises the emphasis in social work training on adult stress as a precipitator of physical abuse of children, rather than an awareness of how the manipulation of violence, particularly by men, is used within the family to impose their will on others (O'Hara, 1992, 4; Bridge Child Care Consultancy Service, 1991, 86).

O'Hara's suggestions for good practice concentrate very much upon using the law to empower women and children to protect themselves. For example, the use of laws relating to occupation of the family home to protect children from violence and emotional abuse associated with violence, and the use of private proceedings to protect children from abuse or abduction when necessary (O'Hara, 1992, 4).

In this respect O'Hara is advocating that professionals involved in child protection make far greater use of what is generally known as the 'domestic violence' legislation. The contrast between the assistance received by women in Women's Aid refuges compared to that provided by social services illustrates why this is imperative. In refuges the law is used to help women to take control of their own lives, and to protect themselves and their children from further violence. Paradoxically many women who seek assistance from social services end up at case conferences discussing whether their children should be registered 'at-risk'. This is not to deny that in some instances agency child protection procedures are appropriate. However, a wider perspective on violence against women allows for choice in the legal strategies adopted by social workers and for a much greater prospect of empowering both women and children. This is the single most important step for future social work practice in this field.

In Britain there are changes taking place in family law which increase the focus on children's rights and lessen parents' rights over children. These changes are embodied in the Children Act 1989 and in recent recommendations by the Law Commission entitled *Family Law, Domestic Violence and Occupation of the Family Home* (Law Commission, 1992), which have been accepted by Government and are currently being debated in Parliament. Such developments open a window of opportunity for social workers.

The Law Commission's recommendations stem largely from an implicit recognition of the effects on children of witnessing violence against women and the relationship between violence against women and some forms of abuse of children (O'Hara, 1992, 4). There are a range of recommendations which would increase the court's power to: oust the violent partner; transfer tenancies to the non-abusing parent; exclude named individuals from the child's home (Law Commission, 1992, 59-60). At the heart of these proposals is the desire to strengthen the legal position of the non-abusing parent in order to protect their children.

O'Hara believes that implementation of the Law Commission's recommendations would *"go a long way towards enabling the courts to recognise the links between child abuse and domestic violence and to make provisions accordingly for the protection of children"* (O'Hara, 1992, 5). These changes would also have to be followed by a change in judicial attitudes to create a much wider awareness of the nature of violence against women. However, these proposals are not without their drawbacks.

Having to encourage women to return to the home in which they have only recently been abused is likely to mean that they continue to live in fear for a considerable period of time. The effects of this on the women and children involved, even if further violent episodes do not occur, is immeasurable. (Charles, 1991, 55)

Whilst legislative reforms are a welcome addition in empowering women and children, the need for supportive aftercare work by both refuge workers and social workers would become critical.

Children's rights

There is little reference made in the above discussion to the views or wishes expressed by children. *"While children's rights may nominally be the starting point for much of the concern about child abuse, this is rarely explicit and the implications rarely thought through"* (Parton, 1990(i), 23).

Broadly speaking the debate on children's rights has focused on the differences between the 'liberationists' and the 'protectionists' (Parton, 1990(i), 23). The former wish to extend to children a number of rights held exclusively by adults. This would involve children in making decisions about what they want, having more control over their own lives and environments. The protectionist lobby favour restricting children's lives in some areas, whilst compelling them to do certain things, all in their 'best interests'.

Different aspects of the protectionist approach have dominated attitudes and developments in social work response to child abuse. Extending children's rights means attempting to construct a policy and practice that not only listens to children's wishes but acts upon them wherever possible. The Children Act 1989 is encouraging in this respect since in certain circumstances it places a duty on courts and social workers to ascertain the wishes and feelings of children. However, moving from this position to structuring social work practice in a way that genuinely involves children in the decision-making process seems a long way hence. Increasing children's rights has a number of practical implications in relation to children of abused women.

i) Contact arrangements post-separation

The philosophy underlying British legislation is that it is in a child's best interests to know and have contact with both parents post-separation. The Children Act 1989 reinforces this approach. One of the main principles of the Act is to encourage mediation and to reduce conflict between separating couples. The Act has introduced the notion of joint and shared responsibility between parents, replacing custody and access. Whilst this development is welcome, there are concerns that the Act may work against women and children.

In particular, there is a lack of discussion about the effects of violence against women on the separation/divorce process and on child care arrangements. Speaking on a recent television programme about this subject a leading family solicitor stated that, "... *in over 200 pages the Children Act manages to avoid ever dealing with the issue of domestic violence*" (Woodcraft, 1992).

On the same television programme Mr Justice Johnson, a senior High Court Judge, echoed the view that children are best served by continued contact with both parents post-separation, even in cases of children who have witnessed violence against their mothers. Widely regarded as one of the more 'sympathetic' judges towards abused women and children, he argued,

I think that one of the most damaging things to children is that sometimes the consequences of violence between parents means that they are cut-off from one of their parents ... I am not concerned with the rights of the parent to see the child, I am more concerned that the child has a right to see their absent parent. (Johnson, 1992)

In some cases it seems that professionals view a child's right to contact visits with an absent parent as a right that the child cannot refuse (O'Hara, 1990, 4). O'Hara cites a number of examples from her work at the Children's Legal Centre to illustrate this point. Women have been threatened with contempt of court, imprisonment, care proceedings and the transfer of custody to the father by courts in order to enforce access arrangements that children do not want. "*Such an approach twists concepts*

34

of children's rights and uses them to rob children of any real autonomy and of respect for their wishes and feelings" (O'Hara, 1990, 17).

As I discussed in the previous chapters the effects upon children of violence against women may not cease at separation. Hester and Radford assert that,

... if we are to take the interests of children seriously, then we have to take into account that where the father is violent towards the mother, children are likely to be adversely affected when they see their fathers. We have to consider that responsibility for children by fathers in these circumstances could be detrimental to the child's health and well-being. (Hester and Radford, 1992, 60)

For example, in cases of child sexual abuse there is considerable clinical evidence that men sometimes use sophisticated psychological 'triggers' to continue abusing children when physical contact is not possible. Informal access arrangements, which usually involve family members who lack knowledge of these techniques, leave children especially vulnerable to this form of abuse (O'Hara, 1990, 17-18).

Most importantly, it is essential that social workers increase the rights of children to have a meaningful say in decisions about their future. Often the views of children are not even sought, let alone taken into consideration. The report into the death of Sukina discussed earlier lamented the fact that Sukina's views were not heard. Little weight was given to her stated fears about her dad or her requests to be looked after, nor were her explanations of violence against her taken seriously (Bridge Child Care Consultancy Service, 1991, 80).

For children who wish to continue seeing their fathers the issue of violence against women poses serious dilemmas. It is sometimes assumed that women will automatically obstruct access arrangements because of their hostility to ex-partners (Hester and Radford, 1992, 62). This has not been the case in general and it was not the case for my research participants. The Hester and Radford study found that mothers generally resisted contact only when children did not want it, or in situations where the child was patently suffering. Significantly, some women resisted access by fathers due to problems concerning the safety of their children.

35

*If mum and me met Dad on a Sunday afternoon there would be six or seven women from the refuge dotted around the gardens of the pub. Its great the other women were supporting her like that - he never knew they were there! But I know this may sound funny, I really think that's wrong. I really think there should've been someone else there of authority because he was **such a** violent man. It seemed the outside world didn't give a shit.* (Clara)

A major concern for women has been the lack of adequate supervision in cases of violence against women. *"Both the safety of women and the welfare of children in our study were frustrated by the lack of facilities to support access arrangements"* (Hester and Radford, 1992, 63). For example, there is evidence from women leaving refuges that during access visits men use their children to continue to harass, intimidate and control their former partners (O'Hara, 1992, 4; Hester and Radford, 1992, 61).

These difficulties are likely to escalate. The increased emphasis in the Children Act 1989 on informal arrangements, negotiation and mediation in post-separation child care arrangements ignores the power imbalances between family members that leave women and children vulnerable to abuse. Finding ways to facilitate contact without jeopardising the safety of children and women is clearly problematic. A shift in priorities within social work towards more support services for women and children may be especially important in these situations. Helping women to facilitate well-defined, supervised access arrangements may be an important step in empowering children who wish to continue seeing their fathers whilst simultaneously trying to ensure the safety and well-being of both children and women.

ii)   Improving social work intervention with child witnesses
There is a dearth of intervention strategies designed specifically for children of abused women. Even in the USA and Canada, where there has been more research and consequently much greater awareness of the need, mandatory interventions through legislation, such as reporting responsibilities and required investigations, are vague or non-existent. For example, in Canada only two provinces out of ten make specific reference in their child welfare legislation that children who witness what they describe as 'violence in their family' may be in need of protection (Jaffe, Wolfe and Wilson, 1990, 103).

Raising the profile of violence against women as an issue on social work qualifying courses may be an important starting point. Identification is the key to assisting child witnesses as it is the key to assisting women. Qualified staff should also have the opportunity for regular in-service training to ensure that violence against women retains a high profile in policy and practice. For example, in Denmark trainee teachers are placed with refuge children's workers to experience working with children who have been abused through violence against women (Hester and Radford, 1992, 69). There is scope for this idea to be developed in this country on social work qualifying courses.

Furthermore, there is a need to challenge racist assumptions prevalent in some social work departments that violence and abuse is an accepted part of black culture and way of life (Bogle, 1988, 134; Hudson, 1992, 142; Mama, 1989). *"They further perpetuate stereotypes of black families and they carry the danger that black children who are abused will remain vulnerable as a result of professional inaction"* (Hudson, 1992, 142). However, there must also be a greater awareness of the impact of statutory intervention upon a black family living in a racist society (Parton, 1990 (ii), 58).

Historically refuges have not encouraged an active role by social services because of their concern about revictimising abused women. Furthermore, refuges may worry that knowledge of a close working relationship between social services and refuges may discourage women from seeking safety in the first instance (Jaffe, Wolfe and Wilson, 1990, 103).

Shelters in the USA and Canada that have been effective in working with child protection agencies on behalf of their clients have suggested a number of interventions. These include: training workshops for staff in each agency on issues surrounding violence against women, including legal mandates and responsibilities, and closer relationships among staff in the two agencies that encourage two-way referrals between the services.

In this country Ball has made important proposals for services to the children of abused women. She argues for training and accreditation agencies to recognise the particular demands and requirements of children's work in refuges, and to devise and make available training packages to meet those demands. Furthermore, she argues for both central and local government to recognise the importance of this training support for children's workers alongside recognition of their role in the network of community care for children at risk (Ball, 1990, 17).

One of the most interesting intervention strategies offered by shelters involves utilising social work staff to offer programmes such as children's groups in refuges. These would enable women and children to encounter social workers as helpers rather than as officials policing abuse. This idea has become practice in one part of America. The Children's Program was established as part of a larger Domestic Abuse Project which supplements shelter services in the USA.

The Program offers a wide range of practical and therapeutic services including open-ended self-help groups, support and education groups to abused women and their children. The most encouraging of these for child witnesses are the groups described in detail by Grusznski, Brink and Edleson (1988). The groupwork focuses upon the support and educational needs of children of abused women over a 10-week period. Briefly, they outline seven major issues: establishing responsibility for the violence; issues of shame and isolation; protection planning for children in violent situations; expression of feelings; conflict resolution; gender role issues; and building self-esteem (Grusznski, Brink and Edleson, 1988, 434).

The most comprehensive example of joint working practice that I discovered comes from Australia and involves Scottish Women's Aid's first National Children's worker, who emigrated to Australia in 1987. The Children and Domestic Violence Group involves representatives from Women's Shelters, the Department for Family and Community Services, Child and Adolescent Mental Health Services, Youth Services and Women's Community Health Centres from across South Australia, working together to eliminate male violence and promote services for children (Children and Domestic Violence Interagency Group, 1992). This powerful force in Australian child services represents a major step forward for both abused women and their children.

In summary, the emphasis within social work practice needs to shift from prioritising family reconciliation towards putting the children's interests first. Clear distinctions need to be made and acknowledged between the abusing and non-abusing parent. Good practice must support and empower women to protect themselves and their children instead of disregarding and trivialising male violence. The law has provision which should be seized to empower and strengthen the position of the non-abusing parent in order to give greater protection to the children.

Furthermore the child's needs must be given a distinct and separate status. It is particularly important that children's wishes are voiced and taken into account when considering contact arrangements. Finally, there is a dearth of policy and practice initiatives in this country for children of abused women. Where possible I have highlighted positive developments from abroad from which we can draw lessons.

SUMMARY OF PART ONE

Much greater attention should be paid to the experiences, perceptions and wishes of the children of abused women. However, the question of how best to help child witnesses cannot be divorced from the need to break the conspiracy of silence that surrounds violence against women. The ideology of the family and the privacy of family life, deeply entrenched within our society , conceals the extent and horrific nature of violence against women. It is vital that professionals and public alike look beyond the closed doors of the family and register the pain and misery of many women and children.

The first priority is to promote a wider awareness of violence against women in the home. Social workers have a major role to play in this process. An understanding of violence against women needs to be incorporated at the centre of social work practice, informing both policy and intervention strategy. This is especially important for black women in this country because prejudice and ignorance about culturally 'acceptable' levels of violence shapes some social work practice.

Social workers are in a powerful position to offer women some of the practical, financial and emotional support they need to escape violent men. In addition, social workers' statutory responsibilities towards children can be used in ways which empower women to protect both themselves and their children.

In many respects feminism has had the most success in challenging male violence. The life-saving role of Women's Aid refuges and the importance of a feminist approach to empowering women has been an enduring feature of the personal accounts of women in these refuges. There is a huge gulf between the services offered by Women's Aid refuges and social services departments to women and children escaping male violence. Both services have a key role to play, therefore this gulf must be bridged.

With few exceptions social work departments in this country have yet to develop fully their understanding of children's experience of violence against women. Similarly there are very few intervention strategies to help children to deal with the effects of male violence. It is vital that both refuge and social workers identify the factors which either reinforce or heal the effects of this experience.

For social workers the impact upon child witnesses of violence against women converges with child protection issues, but in a much broader sense than is currently recognised. Social workers need to take note of the growing body of research which suggests that a great deal of harm may beset children living with years of violence, fear and guilt. There is also growing evidence of the links between violence against women and the emotional, physical and sexual abuse of children.

The shortcomings in refuge provision for children are partly the result of poor funding, lack of resources and entrenchment within the movement as a whole in the current hostile political and economic climate. However, three central issues must be addressed if refuges are to make a fuller contribution towards helping children in refuges.

- Firstly, the numbers and status of children's workers must be raised within refuges. The positive support already offered by children's workers is vital in helping children cope with their experiences.
- Secondly, children's workers themselves also need to develop knowledge and skilled intervention strategies to facilitate this process.
- Finally, there is an urgent need for more co-operation and joint developments between refuges and other progressive organisations.

It is also apparent that whilst concern for children in refuges is considerable, there have been few attempts to document the experiences of these children. I have taken a small step by asking four adults about their experiences of a childhood filled with violence directed against their mothers, and of subsequently living in a women's refuge. Further research in this area would help to give children a voice and the opportunity to influence services created in their interests, together with reducing their sense of isolation and powerlessness within refuges. Whilst research in this area is generally scarce, the almost total lack of documented information about the experiences of children from ethnic minority communities in this country is particularly worrying.

Policy and practice within both refuges and social services departments must be underpinned with a greater adherence to children's rights. In particular the views and wishes of child witnesses must be sought and taken seriously by those making decisions in the child's best interests. In this respect children's meetings within refuges are an encouraging development. They represent the clearest sign of adults facilitating children to speak for themselves. Despite the difficulties this entails, and the generally low priority given to children's views, this kind of imaginative approach should be further encouraged. The burgeoning debate over children's rights may well open up opportunities which will profit social workers seeking to empower women and children to live free from male violence.

PART TWO

WHAT CHILDREN TELL CHILDLINE ABOUT DOMESTIC VIOLENCE
Carole Epstein and Gill Keep

Kath told the ChildLine counsellor that her father kept hitting her mother when he came home drunk. He even hit her mum in front of her three-year-old brother, who gets very upset. Kath was frightened and anxious. She said: "Dad feels he can do what he likes." She didn't know which way to turn. Her call ended abruptly when her dad came into the room.

Joe phoned late one night. That evening his stepdad had beat up his mum, who was nine months pregnant. Joe thought that his stepdad suspected his mum of "trying to lose the baby" because she had started bleeding. Joe was angry and upset and told ChildLine he felt "powerless to stop the violence."

Introduction

For some years there has been a growing awareness about the extent and effects of domestic violence. However, most of the research has focused on the adults involved and very little on the children. Every year, thousands of children witness violence in the home. Some of these live in refuges with their mothers who have left a violent relationship, but many others remain at home. Children are profoundly affected by domestic violence but have had little opportunity to articulate their views and feelings about it. This paper is an attempt to highlight the predicament of these children by conveying their own thoughts and words.

What is ChildLine?
ChildLine is an organisation dedicated to helping children and enabling their voices to be heard. It is a 24-hour national telephone counselling service for children and young people in trouble, need or danger. The service is free and confidential. Since it started in October 1986, it has counselled more than 400,000 children.

Children call ChildLine about all kinds of problems and concerns. Last year, sexual and physical abuse accounted for approximately 27 per cent of calls. But children also called, amongst other things, about family relationships, bullying, pregnancy, problems with friends or partners, worries about sex and running away. For many, speaking to a counsellor at ChildLine is the first time that a child has ever been able to speak of her or his experiences or problems.

ChildLine's information on domestic violence
ChildLine's counselling records provide a rich source of information. ChildLine is unique in having direct communication with large numbers of children who give us their accounts, views and feelings about their predicament. From this information, we can draw authentic testimony. However, it is important to remember that the primary aim of the service is to counsel children and ChildLine's policy is that counselling will be "child led". It follows that some questions which would be helpful for information purposes are not necessarily put to the child. As a result, the information on the counselling records is not "complete". For example, the child may not choose to give us her name, address or age. All names and personal details in the paper are, of course, changed in order to protect the identity of the children.

Between June 1993 - May 1994, ChildLine counsellors spoke to a total of 1,554 children about domestic violence - that is, about 130 children a month. Sometimes the child phoned to talk specifically about domestic violence; but children also phoned, initially wanting to talk about another problem and during the course of the conversation also spoke about violence at home.

The analysis in this chapter is based on a random sample of 126 callers who contacted ChildLine within a period of six months. The majority of the children were between 11 and 15 years old and 91 per cent were girls. The overall ratio of girls to boys calling ChildLine is 4:1. The lower than average percentage of boys calling ChildLine on this issue suggests that it may be even more difficult for boys to call about violence at home than about other issues.

Children's experiences of domestic violence

1. Children's description of domestic violence
Children rarely use the term "domestic violence" when referring to violence in their home. Nonetheless it is clear that their experience is, for the most

part, of men assaulting women. In only three cases out of the 126 examined, did children speak of their mothers hitting their partners. One caller phoned about her grandfather being violent to her grandmother, and another about her aunt and uncle.

Some children phoned, worried about their friends, whose fathers were hitting their mothers. But the overwhelming majority of children (110) spoke about violence to their mother by her partner. Although in most cases the violent man was the biological father, in a large minority of cases (16 per cent) it was the step-father or the mother's boyfriend.

Beth (10 years old) called to say that she saw her father hitting her mother that morning. When her dad saw her watching, he turned on her and told her to get out. Beth left and was too scared to go home.

Daksha's father beat her mother so badly that the police came and took her mother to a refuge. Daksha had not seen her today, was too scared of her dad to go home and phoned ChildLine from a friend's house to ask what she should do.

Occasionally the father no longer lived with the child and mother but still intimidated and assaulted them.

Jack, aged 9, phoned, terrified because his father, who no longer lived with them, had been coming round and smashing their windows. He had started to have terrifying dreams of his father smashing the door down and getting to him and his mother. His mother had tried, unsuccessfully, to get an injunction.

2. When do children call us about domestic violence
For many children who call ChildLine, the violence has been occurring for a long time - months or even years. For some their main preoccupation is another problem and the violence is like a continuous backdrop and only mentioned to the counsellor as an afterthought.

Other children, particularly those who phoned to speak specifically about the violence, called immediately or soon after the event. In a few cases, their father had never hit their mother before, or not for a very long time, and the shock had caused the child to seek help outside the family home by ringing ChildLine.

Lucy phoned very distraught because the previous night she had heard her parents arguing, had gone into the kitchen to discover her father holding a knife to her mum. This had never happened before, and neither parents would talk to her about it, telling her "not to worry". Lucy was desperate to know what was going on, and aged 15, felt she was old enough to be told.

Children phone ChildLine at all times of day and night, but in this study, the most common were between 8.00 a.m. and 9.00 a.m. - before they went to school, and then after school, before bedtime. Six children phoned after midnight and before 7.00 a.m.

3. Where do children call from?
Children usually phoned from home (32) or from a phone box (44). Other places included friends' houses, boyfriend's house and school.

4. How do children explain/understand the violence?
Some children do not tell us whether or how they understand the causes of the violence, or express an understanding of how it might stop: for them the violence "just was". One caller, for instance, could remember a time when there had been no violence; when there had been family picnics, days out, playing games and lots of laughter - all the more incomprehensible to her, then, that those times had been replaced by times of fear and insecurity.

Domestic violence appears to these children to be inexplicable, a situation which leaves them anxious and confused. They tell ChildLine that they struggle to make sense of the violent behaviour but may be unable to do so. They describe being profoundly alarmed by witnessing adults behaving in ways which appear to them irrational or senseless. Their level of fear and anxiety is increased by the unpredictability of the violent acts. If they cannot predict when violence is likely to occur, they are likely to remain always alert and on their guard, distracted by the ever present possibility of their mother being injured. One young caller talked of how her father's violence affected every aspect of family life to the extent that they all felt that they were "constantly walking on eggs", afraid that the very least thing would bring a violent response.

Some children had clearly tried hard to think what triggered their father's, or step-father's violence. Alcohol, unemployment and loss or bereavement

46

were mentioned. In all, 46 of the children in this study mentioned one of these factors.

Alcohol
Approximately a quarter (33) of all callers mentioned alcohol to the counsellor. In some cases, the connection between violence and alcohol was clear; for example, one caller said that on Friday and Saturday nights, her dad got drunk and hit her mum, but the rest of the week, they all got on okay.

Unemployment/redundancy
Unemployment and redundancy were mentioned by only six callers, representing a small proportion of the calls. In those cases, however, the child saw the unemployment or redundancy as a trigger for the violence, where the father had previously not been violent. One caller said that her dad had been made redundant six months ago and had become very violent but had given up looking for work. The child had taken on the responsibility of looking for jobs for him.

Loss/separation/bereavement
Seven children mentioned a loss or bereavement which appeared to have affected their father's behaviour. In one case, Gina believed that her father had begun to beat her mother more frequently as he was faced with his last child, Gina, leaving home. In another case, Alice's younger sister had died some time ago, and since that time, her father had begun to hit her and her mother. In two cases, the death of the father's beloved pet had appeared, to the child, to have resulted in more violence towards her mother. In these cases, it appears that the loss had precipitated a greater degree of violence, rather than triggering violence, and it appears to have been the increase in violence which caused the child to phone ChildLine.

The effects of domestic violence on children

1. Children's reactions to the violence
> *"I feel so helpless.."*
> *"I'd like to kill him.."*
> *"I think he hates me.."*
> *"If mum won't deal with him, then I will. I have to stay strong to hold things together."*

"Dad behaves like a mad dog.."

"I am ashamed of him - I can't tell anyone because then they will know I haven't got a proper dad.."

"I feel like killing myself..""I'm really scared he's going to start hitting me and my brother and sisters..."

"I'd rather run away than go home.."

"My dad is a power maniac.."

"I hate my dad and I want to leave home..."

"There's nothing I can do..."

"I've only seen the violence once but I'm scared things are going to get worse.."

"My friends don't want to listen anymore - it's been going on for too long -I've become a broken record..."

"I want some peace for myself.."

"I used to get upset - now I feel angry.."

"I sit in my room and cry.."

"At times he can be really nice and at times he's like an animal.."

"It's affecting my school work.."

These comments demonstrate that children are able to speak directly about how they feel to ChildLine and can articulate the intensity of their responses to the violence they witness. They talk of being scared, confused, upset, frightened, angry, distraught, sad, suicidal, guilty, helpless, betrayed, ashamed, powerless. However, children do not always tell us how they cope with the burden of the painful feelings they describe.

Many children at some times in their lives will face a crisis or danger which evokes a similar range of feelings and of stress. For most, the crisis is external to their immediate family and is a specific event which passes. The child is then in a position to recover and to use those closest to her to help the process of recovery. The situation is very different when the danger is within the home, when it is repeated over and over, and when those closest to the child cannot help her recover. Children tell ChildLine that their feelings towards the violent partner will usually prevent them approaching him for solace and understanding, and their concern and desire to protect their mother also interferes with their ability to ask for help from her.

Previous research (for example Black (1993); Jaffe, Wolfe & Wilson (1990)) has identified and discussed common physical and behavioural symptoms suffered by children who witness domestic violence. These include

48

depression, anxiety, hyperactivity, difficulties with concentration, eating problems, aggression and some medical symptoms such as asthma. Callers to ChildLine help to confirm these findings. They describe, for example, being unable to concentrate at school or being unable to sleep.

Sometimes children are aware of the link between the violence and what is happening to them, but others are unable to connect their own physical suffering or behaviour with the violence they are witnessing.

2. Children feel responsible

Dan, aged 16, sounded "almost breathless he was so stressed" when he phoned. His mother had just gone to hospital as a result of his dad's violence. His two siblings had been sent to relatives, and he, Dan, was waiting for his dad to come back from the pub. He had stayed at home to stop his father making trouble at his relatives' house. Dan talked about how he was the buffer between his dad and everyone else and how he was worried that his mum would be discharged from hospital to their home to face his dad on her own.

Dan saw himself as a "piggy in the middle" - a feeling which was echoed by several children. In addition to their own powerful and confusing feelings, the children who call us feel responsible in very many ways for the situation at home. They feel they should try to stop the violence when it is occurring and may actually try to intervene physically or verbally.

In this way, the young people are taking responsibility for protecting their mothers, even though it may well put them at great risk of being hurt themselves. Young people have explicitly said to ChildLine: "I'd rather he hit me than my mum". It is as if they are saying to us that it is easier to bear the physical pain of being hurt than the emotional pain of knowing that someone they love is being injured and being unable to prevent it.

As well as trying to stop their fathers at the time of violence, children try to protect their mothers by offering practical help or advice. Some ask ChildLine to provide them with information, such as the phone number of a women's refuge, so that they can pass this on to their mother. Children describe making suggestions to their mothers, encouraging them to leave or separate from their partners, suggesting they report the violence. However, such concern is not always acknowledged or appreciated by the mother herself. It can be confusing and hurtful to a child when their mother does not accept or act on the advice she gives.

Callers also describe feeling responsible for causing the arguments and violence, and for the ambivalent and antagonistic feelings their parents have towards each other. They may feel that their very presence is an added burden or that their demands are excessive. One caller told ChildLine that her birth had caused the violence because she had used up all her parents' money; another caller described her father becoming violent when he felt her mother had given her more attention than him.

This type of situation escalates dangerously as the child is often the one person to whom the mother can turn for sympathy and understanding. The mother-child relationship becomes intense and important and this, in turn, can be seen by the child as provoking further violence from the father.

Children tell us how parents unwittingly confirm the child's sense of being responsible for causing the violence by arguing about the child within her hearing. Disputes regarding discipline, child care or education, for example, can all be interpreted by the child as: "I am the cause of the conflict and therefore the violence."

Feeling responsible for violence between adults is an enormous burden for children to carry. It is particularly overwhelming because in reality children are powerless in this situation. They tell us they feel, and are, helpless; they cannot be as strong and as powerful as their fathers, they cannot force their mothers to act. Yet they feel guilty for not being more effective in trying to protect their mothers, especially as they are aware that no one else will act because no one else knows or believes what is going on, so the responsibility falls back on them.

3. Relationships with parents
One of the most disturbing aspects of witnessing domestic violence for children is the confusion they feel about their parents, and the distortions forced on their relationships with them. The children's need to be children - to be looked after, nurtured, protected and allowed to take risks - appears to have been fundamentally undermined by their home situation. Children talking to us have been forced into inappropriate and pseudo-mature relationships with one or both parents, often assuming a parental role towards their siblings.

Relationship with mother

An overwhelming impression of wishing to protect and help their mother comes through from the children's calls, but with that, often a deep frustration when the mother is unable or unwilling to leave or confront her partner. Many children called wanting to talk about how they could help their mother, and would talk only reluctantly about the effect of the violence on them. Many were angry and hurt about their mother's sufferings and empathised deeply with her. Ruth, for example, talked of how she and her sister lay awake at nights listening to her parent's arguments, and worrying that her mum would get hit again.

Sometimes the love for their mother was mixed with a feeling of disappointment with her - disappointment at being "weak" or a "victim"; of not standing up for herself or protecting herself or her children, including the caller, from the violence. Callers often expressed intense frustration when their mother either refused to acknowledge the violence, or played it down, by saying, for example, that they were "playing games", or saying, after a particularly vicious attack: "don't worry, I'm okay."

Similarly, children felt betrayed when their mother took the father's side or defended him. In one case, the caller's mother accused her of trying to break up the family when she tried to talk to her mother about the violence. She said: *"I just want me and my mum to stick together against my dad."*

The feeling of betrayal was particularly acute when the mother hit the child - as one child said: *"My dad hits my mum, and she takes it out on me."* Children who may well have positive and negative feelings about their fathers become very confused if the violent behaviour is seen to be condoned by their mothers. This can be experienced as a rejection of the child's concern and caring for their mother.

Many children said that they wanted their parents to divorce or separate. But often they felt guilty and ashamed of that wish. Others were desperate for their parents not to split up: one caller, physically abused herself by her father, was adamant that she did not want her parents to divorce.

Some callers talked of giving up on their mother, of leaving home, running away, and abandoning her because of her inability to change. A total of 17 out of 126 children said they had either run away, or had seriously considered it.

Alice, for example, phoned in the early hours of the morning, desperate to move out of the house, but feeling very guilty at the thought of deserting her mother. She had "tried everything I know to persuade mum to leave", but without success. She could stand it no longer.

Relationship with father
Children's feelings about their father were also deeply ambivalent. Many talked of hating him, and wishing he would just go away, out of their lives. They believed that once he went, life would be better, and they would get on well with their mum again. Many talked of despising him.

Children also spoke of still loving their father or wanting to be able to love him, but not being able to do so. Some expressed anguish at not being able to give the love they wanted to their father. One caller, for example, said: *"I love my mum's boyfriend, but I just want him to stop hitting my mum".* She was afraid to talk to him about it, in case it provoked him and she felt that the violence was her fault to some extent, because she said she was *"a problem child".*

Relationship with others
The children who call describe the violence occurring within small, closed family units. They describe little, if any, contact with extended family members. Occasionally children do talk to an aunt, uncle or grandparents, but describe them as equally helpless, able only sometimes to offer a temporary respite for the children.

Domestic violence is usually a family secret, with much effort expended in maintaining the secret. It appears that the parents, fearing their situation will become known outside the family, limit their own friendships so that few other adults come into the child's life. Parents also fear that the child will betray them by speaking to their own friends and so these relationships are often limited or forbidden completely. Emily, aged 10, was forbidden by her mother to see her friends as *"she didn't want me to talk about our problems at home."*

Even when children are allowed contact with others, the pressure of having to keep secrets and their constant anxiety about home life interferes with the development of ordinary peer relationships. It is ordinary behaviour for children to share details of their home life, but this is dangerous for children who carry the secret of domestic violence. If they relax with their friends they may forget to be on guard - they may let something slip. Children say it is easier to be alone than to take this risk.

Because of their isolation children are often unable to think of anyone to whom they can turn or whom they can trust. This is similar to the position described by children who are physically or sexually abused. They feel that no one will understand or believe them. In reality they may not have had the opportunity to develop the social skills and relationships which teaches them how to communicate effectively and how to be heard. Not only may there be no one to tell - the children don't know how to tell.

Summary
Witnessing domestic violence has a profound effect on children and young people. The children who call ChildLine clearly describe the painful emotional responses and physical and behavioural symptoms which have been shown to be connected to witnessing violence in the home. They describe isolated lives and disturbed relationships with their parents. They describe feeling responsible both for causing the violence and for preventing it and this in turn engenders an overwhelming sense of helplessness.

Domestic violence and physical abuse

Thirty eight per cent (48) of our sample of children calling ChildLine about domestic violence talked of their mother's partner physically abusing them and or their siblings. Children talk of being "hit", "beaten", "whipped". They describe being hit with slippers, belts, pokers, bottles, furniture and bats, and of being banged against the wall or stairs.

Isobel came on the phone in the early hours of the morning crying and crying - the counsellor could hardly hear her. Gradually she calmed down and was able to speak. She said she couldn't go home any more. Her father was beating her mother, herself and her brothers. As well as beating them, he made them stand in a room and didn't let them leave without his permission. Isobel was so scared at the thought of going home that she would not contact the police or social services for fear they would send her back.

In very many of these cases, children called ChildLine to talk about their own physical abuse; their mother's abuse by the father was an additional piece of information. Earlier studies, notably the report into the death of Sukina Hammond in 1988, pointed to the strong links between child abuse and violence towards the mother - in that particular case, the failure of social services to pay attention to the violence of Sukina's father towards her mother led to Sukina being allowed home, with tragic consequences. Subsequent studies have reinforced the connections (Farmer and Owens 1993).

Children describe physical abuse towards themselves and their mothers in the context of arguments and conflict within the home. Family life is described as disruptive and chaotic: children talk of absent parents, lack of predictability and security about basic needs such as meals or general care. Violence in the home for these children is yet another seemingly arbitrary event.

Devina, aged 13, phoned begging us to get her dad to leave home. He had already been in court for physical abuse, but was now back living with her mum, brother and herself. Her mum had left and gone with the children into bed and breakfast which Devina said was "horrible". In the end her mum came back home. Devina just wanted her dad to leave them in peace.

Where do children seek help?

It may seem surprising at first glance that so many children find it almost impossible to ask for help. The children who call us describe why this might be so: they are often, like children who are abused, trapped in a domestic environment which is constructed around secrecy and lies. Children witness lies and secrecy as a normal part of everyday life and are participants in that process. One caller told us of having to tell lies at school about her bruises. Another, and this recurred regularly, colluded with her mother in pretending to the outside world that nothing was wrong at home. In some cases, the child and the mother lied about the violence, because the perpetrator, the father, was a respected member of the community - one caller's father, for example, was a solicitor, another ran a local business and was known and respected by the local community. Constantly denying the reality of their day to day lives deepened, for the children, their sense of confusion, isolation and of being trapped.

Like children who are abused, children who have disclosed violence in the home face disbelief and denial. The result can be to drive them further into isolation, making them increasingly sceptical about the possibility of being helped.

Telling someone at school

Telling a teacher at school can be problematic for the child. Some of the callers to ChildLine had colluded with their mothers in lying to their teachers; speaking to that teacher about the abuse then seemed an impossible task.

Some children had managed to tell someone at school. Both Mandy and Alex spoke to ChildLine from the school secretary's office - in one case, the school secretary then coming on the phone to speak to the counsellor. The school had, in those instances, felt able to provide a safe place for the child to talk.

However, in other cases, the response was not so helpful. One caller was told by her teacher: *"I can't believe it that such a nice father would behave like that - you're just upset because your mother has married him"*. Another caller was told by his head teacher that he must come to terms with his parents' problems. When another child, Alan, told his teacher, his teacher promptly told his father, who then beat him. When Alan called us, he had not been to school since.

School is a very important potential source of support for all children. It is crucial that information and training on the effects of domestic violence is made available to teaching and non-teaching staff in schools. Much work has been done in past years in clarifying the school's role in relation to child abuse and child protection. The issue of domestic violence could be very usefully included in these areas of concern.

Telling other agencies

Other agencies were already involved in just a few cases, although there may have been involvement not mentioned by callers. Seven callers said that the police had been called in the past by the mother and twice an injunction had been sought. One caller described how, the day after the injunction expired, her father returned to stand outside the house, hammering on the door for twenty minutes. This continued about four times a week, until she and her siblings felt like "hostages" in their own home, afraid to go out.

In most cases, secrecy and fear of the consequences had prevented the family from reporting the violence to the police. Another caller told us her father had threatened to "break her legs" if she told the police about his abuse of her mother.

The lack of involvement by social services was even more noticeable. In only four of the cases involving physical abuse of the *child* did the caller mention social services involvement. Six children phoned to ask to be taken into care. When they had talked to the counsellor for a while, it became clear that being taken into care appeared to the child to be the only route out of an impossible life at home.

Some children responded positively to counsellors' suggestions that social services should be contacted. Others were more suspicious and anxious that they would be taken away from other members of the family. One caller, in fact, who already had a social worker, refused to tell him about the violence at home. Another response by callers was: *"I don't want to get my parents into trouble."*

Twice, callers told ChildLine that their mothers had contacted Women's Aid. Counsellors also gave information to callers about getting in touch with Women's Aid.

How do ChildLine counsellors help?

Children living with domestic violence are often terrified of the consequences of telling, and convinced that they will not be believed. When children phone ChildLine, it may be the first time they have even talked about what they are witnessing - what is happening to them, and how they feel about it.

ChildLine offers children the opportunity of being heard and believed - a new experience for many callers. Children are informed that when they speak to ChildLine, the call is confidential, and that no action will be taken without their consent unless their lives are in danger.

Children who are prepared to take the risk discover that they can talk about their lives without losing control of the consequences: no one will be told, nor will more violence occur as a result of them telling. Being heard and believed and taken seriously allows the child to build a trusting relationship with the ChildLine counsellor. Frequently counsellors can help the child acknowledge how responsible they feel for difficulties at home, for protecting their mother, or even for abuse inflicted on themselves. Children are helped to understand that ChildLine does not share this view, and are encouraged to think about allowing others to help them.

The experience of speaking to a counsellor can enable a child subsequently to turn to someone within her own network and risk telling again - now with more faith that she will be understood and believed. ChildLine counsellors will help children think about and rehearse the best way to approach others, to ensure that they are taken seriously.

Children call ChildLine once or more times and may need a few calls before they feel trusting enough to share their experiences and think about what possible action can be taken. Counsellors will also liaise with other professionals and explore what assistance is available for individual children.

Occasionally, children themselves comment on whether ChildLine has been helpful to them. Here is one boy's story:

Simon, aged 14, phoned ChildLine, feeling "very upset and scared" because his dad was hitting and beating his mum. He felt confused when his mum took his dad's side because she was scared. He couldn't talk about it at school, and his family were not in touch with other relatives. He felt alone and isolated. The ChildLine counsellor helped him to talk about his feelings and offered him support. She was able to give him advice about child protection and its implications, as well as information about a local drop-in counselling centre. At the end of the call, Simon commented: "It was really hard for me to phone ChildLine - it took me several goes before I could do it - but I am really glad that I have. I feel that I have taken a step..."

The children who phoned ChildLine to talk about violence in the home were the ones who found, within themselves, both the courage and the opportunity to speak to someone outside their immediate family circle. They phoned, despite their fear of the consequences. There are many thousands of children - particularly young children - who cannot make that initial contact.

CHILDREN IN REFUGES - THE PICTURE NOW
Thangam Debbonaire

This chapter is intended to pick up some of the issues raised by Alex Saunders about work with children in refuges, and give information about current provision. It will try to show how the work done in Women's Aid with children has developed over the years. Epstein and Keep have provided a powerful reflection on the views of children living with violence. Women's Aid has been listening to children's voices in refuges for over two decades. This has provided knowledge and understanding of many of the experiences children leaving domestic violence have, and needs arising out of those experiences. What this section will attempt to do is provide information about how that work has developed and where it is now. This will also include a review of how current provision and practice in social work, court welfare work and housing and benefits legislation are affecting children leaving violence today.

Women's Aid and refuges

Alex Saunders has described elsewhere in this book some of the development of Women's Aid refuges in the 1970s. Other information about this work can be found in Domestic Violence: Action for Change by Malos and Hague (1992). There are now approximately 214 autonomous refuge groups operating in England, many with more than one refuge. There are about 30 in Wales and 40 in Scotland, and six already open in Northern Ireland, with more in development. Refuges exist to provide emergency temporary accommodation, support, information and advice to any woman and her children experiencing violence in the home. They provide this service to women who never come to live in a refuge as well as to residents. Most refuges also provide some form of support for women after they have left the refuge.

Current levels of refuge provision specifically for children

Of the 214 refuges in England, over 75% employ at least one children's worker (Ball, 1994). In the groups which employ a children's worker, an average of 39.2 hours per week is spent on activities relating to children. Most refuges have a playroom, 80% have an outdoor play area. Many groups now employ more than one children's worker. About half of refuge groups provide some form of counselling for children. Most organise excursions and holidays for children who live in or have lived in the refuge and would like to extend this service to other children experiencing domestic violence. A significant minority (23%) provide organised workshops for children. This level of improvement since the children in Alex Saunders' chapter were in refuge can be traced to several factors.

Why specific work with children in refuges?

Women with children very rarely leave their home without their children. Of the 45,000 people who were accommodated in a refuge in England at some time during the financial year 1993-4, nearly 28,000 were children (Ball, 1994). For many women it is an attack or threats directed at their children that finally prompts them to take the first step to leave. Refuges have always provided accommodation for children. Children have talked to refuge staff and volunteers about their own feelings and what has happened to them. Over the years there has been a developing knowledge about the specific experiences of children, as distinct from their mothers, and specific needs arising out of them. The first need for independent advocacy for children therefore comes out of their situation - they are living in a refuge at a time of crisis for themselves and their mother.

The second need arises because many of the children will have been abused themselves. Links between the abuse of women and the abuse of children have been identified both through experience of working with children and listening to them and through research. Two separate pieces of research carried out in 1988 (Stark and Flitcraft, Bowker et al) examined the relationship between the existence of child abuse in a family and the existence of woman abuse and found clear links. (See also Kelly 1994, and Mullender and Morley, 1994 for an overview of the research in this area). Many women working in refuges found that children began to tell about abuse they had also suffered, once they realised that the refuge was a safe to place to tell. This can often take a long time. Often the children have never told anyone else before, or have tried to tell in the past and not been believed. This can be very hard on both children and mothers and a skilled and experienced children's support worker can help them through this time.

Another aspect to the impact of abuse in the home on children is their involvement in the abuse their mother is suffering. Children can and do frequently get caught up in attacks on their mothers in a variety of ways. Accounts from abusers (See Yllö and Bograd 1988) confirm the knowledge we have about this from children themselves. They can be threatened, or blamed for an attack, try to intervene to protect their mother, have toys or pets destroyed, have to call the police and sometimes appear as witnesses in prosecutions. Some children arc conceived as a result of marital rape or damaged while still in the womb. Many will hear or see attacks, and have to live with the effects of the stress and isolation their mother is under, as well as the ever present threat of further violence and the tension this causes.

Sometimes children do not understand what is happening or do not agree with their mother's decision to leave. Sometimes children's wishes and mother's conflict badly. At these times, it is important for a child to have someone clearly identified to support them This advocacy role is one most children's workers have.

Finally, as Gill Keep and Carole Epstein have already described, domestic violence can and does have a profound effect on children and young people. Experience in Women's Aid and research done in Canada (Jaffe et al., 1990) confirm that those effects can last a long time and show themselves in different ways. Providing support services for children can greatly help mediate those effects by assisting the children in coming to terms with their experiences and starting to feel safer and more positive about their lives.

Factors influencing the development of work with children in refuges

Described above and elsewhere in this book are some of the reasons for providing services for children in refuges: they are usually there with their mothers, they have had experiences of their own living with violence, they may have been abused themselves, and sometimes they need independent advocacy distinct from their mothers. Additional factors have influenced the scope and quantity of the development over the years.

One crucial factor is the development of knowledge in the refuge movement about children's experiences, needs and ways of working with them. This knowledge is facilitated by the tradition of networking and sharing information that is still an integral feature of the Women's Aid network. This helps refuges to learn quickly from each other's experience.

There has also been an increase in public attention to children's rights generally, and to the abuse of children. Women in refuges had always known about the abuse children suffered, sexual and physical as well as emotional and neglect, but many outside agencies and the public were unwilling or unable to accept what had been happening within the family all along but previously never spoken about. ChildLine became a famous national institution, which made acknowledgement of children's suffering even harder to avoid. As awareness increased outside Women's Aid, it became easier for refuge groups and for Women's Aid Federation England nationally to make the case to funders and others that children living with domestic violence have specific needs.

There have also been and still are pressures from within and outside refuges for children to be treated as a community responsibility and for mothers to be supported better. The passing of legislation emphasising partnership between local authorities and families and trying to support families to stay together rather than have children taken into care has also helped to focus public and professional attention on the needs of children.

Funding opportunities profoundly influence the development of new work. Funding sources have come from unexpected directions. A small chunk of money came from the government through the National Council of Voluntary Child Care Organisations in 1989 to fund pilot projects for children's workers in refuges which did not already employ them. When this funding ran out, Women's Aid Federation England fund-raisers were able to persuade Children In Need that this was work worth supporting and developing, and they agreed to part fund 7 posts and the National Children's Officer post. Positive evaluations from Ball (1990), (see also this volume, Part I for some valid criticism of this work) encouraged the charity to make this funding more widely available.

Over the last three years, many refuges have been able to employ children's workers on a more secure basis, sometimes on three-year funding agreements. This gives the children's worker a chance to develop the work and her skills and pay closer attention to meeting children's needs, instead of having to fit children's work in with other work and fund-raising for children's activities. Sadly, the awareness raised and the work done have rarely been supported by statutory funding for work with children in refuges. Ball in her most recent evaluation of refuge childwork stated that:

"Children in refuges could clearly be defined as 'in need' under section 17 of the Children Act"

However, most local authorities remain unwilling or unable to provide the money needed for the work with children.

Values and policy behind the work

"Women's Aid exists for the benefit of all women and children experiencing physical, mental or sexual abuse in their relationships. We offer information, advice, access to temporary accommodation, ongoing support and aftercare.

Women's Aid recognises that violence against women results from the unequal position of women in society. We are opposed to all forms of emotional and physical violence and abuse against women and children."
(WAFE statement of Aims and Principles)

Our country's provision for children is relatively low compared to other European countries and this is reflected in current levels of provision for play, child care, nursery education, parental leave from employment for birth and sickness of children, transport, housing, environment and so on. (See Bradshaw, 1990). Understanding of the needs and experiences of children who experience domestic violence is also extremely low, partly because of lack of research and publicity in this area up till now. Women's Aid work with children is therefore informed by this perspective and Women's Aid children's workers believe that children need special time, space and validation of their experiences.

Refuges affiliated to Women's Aid Federation England have a policy of promoting non-violence in refuges for all residents including children. This means that refuge workers work with the mothers and children to promote alternative forms of discipline.

Women's Aid Federation England also has a further national policy on children's rights in refuges which covers provision, protection and participation for children in refuges. A copy of this policy is available or included in the pack of briefing papers on children. Key principles in the policy include: play and fun are healing and part of a child's development; a child in a refuge should have access to independent advocacy and support wherever possible.

Types of work being done with children in Women's Aid groups

There is no single job description that reflects the range of work going on with children in refuges but most children's workers will provide all or some of the following:

- Play sessions for different age groups, including painting and other messy play, cooking
- Outdoor activities e.g. trips to park and further afield
- Holidays for children, e.g. outward bound, outings to seaside, camping in France
- Provision of advice and information specifically for children
- Encouraging and helping children to help each other, through developing peer support, holding separate children's meetings, discussions on refuge rules e.g. why women only
- One to one support sessions with children
- Group support sessions for children
- Organising parties for birthdays and religious festivals
- Holiday play and activity schemes
- Work with mothers and children on a range of matters: problems in parent-child relationships, non violent punishment
- Information on local advice and counselling services, youth and sporting activities etc.
- Advocacy supporting women in getting school and nursery places, access to health care for children, statements for children with special needs
- Involvement in case conferences or giving evidence in court in support of child/mother
- Liaison with local schools about general domestic violence issues, confidentiality, security

How the work is done

Most refuges now have at least one part time children's worker. Some refuges have more, but the posts are in the main part time, the worst funded and insecure in the refuge, which makes planning difficult. It also means that a lot of time has to be spent fund-raising, to pay for activities and staff. The Children Act places a requirement on local authorities to fund work with "children in need", but only half a dozen in the country have taken this on fully. (For further details of current funding issues see below.)

Women's Aid Federation England's National Children's Officer monitors the effects of current legislation and provision on children experiencing domestic violence and represents children's needs and experiences to central government and other national voluntary and statutory agencies including police and probation services, and national children's charities. She also provides resources, information, support and training for children's support workers in refuges.

Continuing development of work with children in refuges

Children's workers do not all work to the same job descriptions or have the same skills. Most provide information about counselling services outside the refuge, some are starting to provide their own counselling for children. Group work is growing as a means of developing children's understanding of their own experiences and helping each other get through them and learn from them. Peer support between children in refuges is often strong, which can be vital to their well being at a time of intense change in their lives. Some refuge children's workers organise workshops for young people and children on different subjects such as bullying, racism and safety skills.

At the time of writing, a few refuge groups are developing outreach and aftercare work for children not living in the refuge. The skills and knowledge are there, the limitations are mostly those of lack of funds. Some refuges are developing counselling services for children. Others have been able to secure funds for play therapy work as distinct from support and advocacy.

Current funding issues

Most funding is unstable, despite a requirement on local authorities to fund work with children in need, and a duty on them to avoid the need for residential care wherever possible. Children in refuges are clearly in need: most are homeless as a result of violence, a significant proportion have been abused, all of them have experienced the effects of living in a violent situation. Many women are still pressurised by social workers into coming into refuges by implicit or explicit threats of removing children or placing them on the at risk register. The cost of keeping a children in care is greater, in both human and financial terms than the cost of supporting a non-abusing parent to care for her children in safety. In 1991-2 the average cost of keeping a child in care was £12,889 per child (Hansard, 11 May 1994, Col 155-6). However, only a tiny minority of local authorities fund work specifically for children in refuges. Allowances from housing associations under the Special Needs Management Allowance system fail even to take into account the basic cost of providing physical space and furniture for children, let alone the cost of staff.

For the large part, refuge work with children still depends on BBC Children In Need. At the time of writing, the charity is understandably keen to decrease this dependency. Women's Aid refuges and WAFE nationally are working to get more statutory support for this much needed and valuable work.

As mentioned above the Children Act requires local authorities to fund or provide services for "children in need". Recent research from NCH Action for Children (1994) clearly identifies that children experiencing domestic violence come under this heading. For those children whose mothers have left the violence, they are additionally in need because they are homeless. Mog Ball's evaluation of work with children in six refuges (Ball, 1992) recommends that work with children in refuges be funded under this heading. Her more recent report into the funding of all refuge services reiterates this recommendation (Ball, 1994).

This most recent evaluation of all refuge work found that £50 million is needed immediately for refuges. This is to enable them to continue to run the full and developing range of services for women and children effectively (Ball, 1994). There is no sign that that sum is forthcoming from statutory sources and money for new developments is scarce.

Effects of agency practice on children leaving violence

Housing

The Housing Act 1985 imposes a duty on local authorities to offer permanent housing to women and children escaping domestic violence. The reality is that many women and children are kept waiting for weeks, months and in some cases over a year for permanent housing. In the mean time they have to live in Bed and Breakfast or other temporary accommodation such as refuges, which are not designed for long-term residence. Bed and Breakfasts and other hostels often carry health risks, particularly for young children, as the bathrooms tend to be shared between many families and there is usually no kitchen. The report published in July 1992 from the inter agency working party on domestic violence, convened by Victim Support, of which Women's Aid Federation England was a part, recommended *"Bed and Breakfast provision should only be used for a limited period, preferably in women and children only accommodation. After this, women and children should be moved into self-contained accommodation."* (Victim Support, 1992)

Education

It is becoming increasingly problematic for mothers to obtain school places for children living in temporary accommodation. Even if the children have places it can be difficult to be able to make use of them because of travel costs and practicalities, risk of abduction by father, restrictions on meal times in Bed and Breakfasts and so on. Space or privacy to do school work are limited. Children's education can therefore suffer as a result of living in temporary accommodation. (Clark, 1993)

Court proceedings

Some children become involved in court proceedings if they are witnesses to attacks on their mother. Many other children become the subject of court proceedings after they have left an abusive man, as arrangements for their future are made under the Children Act 1989. This legislation has caused many problems for women and children escaping domestic violence. There is no mention of domestic violence in the act or accompanying guidance and whilst the emphasis in the act on joint decisions and negotiations is laudable in an ideal situation, it is completely inappropriate when there is violence involved. Indeed it may be dangerous.

There have been numerous cases of women being forced by court welfare officers to have joint meetings with their abuser (see Barron, Harwin and Singh, 1992). This ignores the woman's safety needs. It does not allow her to take part fully and safely in decisions about her children. This is totally contrary to their probation service's own guidance, in the Association of Chief Officers of Probation statement on Domestic Violence (Association of Chief Officers of Probation, 1989). Since the development of these guidelines in 1989 there has been considerable attention paid to this issue by the court welfare profession and improvements are being felt.

A common assumption made in Children Act proceedings where the child expresses a wish to limit or cease contact with her father is that the child's mother has pressurised her to say that. The child may have perfectly good reasons for her wishes. There is also a problem of a lack of safe access centres where contact between children and fathers can take place without threatening the safety of the mother or children.

Some judges and magistrates have made residence orders requiring children to be returned to the family home to live with their mother's abuser, giving the reason that "refuges are not suitable places for children". This ignores the reasons why the mother had to leave the family home to make a safe life for herself and her children. It also displays ignorance about the nature of refuges, and does not allow for the failure of local authorities to provide permanent accommodation for families leaving abuse.

Social services and police
These have a statutory obligation to protect children and many children in homes where there is domestic violence end up on the "at risk" register because of their father's abuse. The links between domestic violence and child abuse have been noted. Mothers are often blamed for the abuse that their children suffer, when they themselves are receiving similar or worse abuse. Sometimes there seem to be contradictions between a mother's and a child's wishes. However, despite the difficulties, there are some principles that we could begin to work from in the interests of maintaining the safety of the children and their mother.

Some of these principles have been explored in some detail by Kelly (1994) in her chapter on the interconnectedness of domestic violence and child abuse, in the first UK book about children's experiences of domestic violence (Mullender and Morley (eds.) 1994). These include principles on acknowledging the links between child abuse and domestic violence in practice, by investigating the prescence of one if the other is known. The principle that the best form of child protection is usually with the non-abusing parent can be encompassed in the work of statutory child protection, and will save money. Children also need to learn the skills of non abusive communication as the next generation becomes adult. This can be done in a school setting, but can also take place in other contexts such as youth work, or starting younger, at nursery age.

Effects of violence and cycle of violence

Experience of working with children in Women's Aid leads us to believe that children can be profoundly affected by living with domestic violence, which is often defined as abuse in itself. These effects can last a number of years. However, we see in refuge work that children are very adaptable and strong and with support from adults they can trust, particularly their mother but also refuge children's workers and other residents, they develop an increased awareness of the damage that violence can do. They also usually gain increased feelings of security, perhaps for the first time feeling safe. As they get older this often translates into a new resilience and determination to do more than simply survive, and a positive determination that violence will not be part of their future life.

Some people wrongly believe that young people can be caught in a cycle of violence and are likely to repeat the behaviour they have witnessed, simply because they have witnessed it. This theory ignores the gender divisions that exist in our society and the other influences on men to maintain control over women. It offers men who abuse an excuse for their behaviour. It denies the experience of the majority of children survivors abuse who do not go on to be abusers themselves. It does not examine the process of leaving the abuse and the healing effects this will usually have on children in the long term especially when given proper help and support. Research in this area has been contradictory and flawed and does not provide us with evidence for the existence of such a cycle. Mullender and Morley (1994) provide a critique of the relevant research. They identify major flaws in methodology (pp 35-36) and conclude that:

"Looking for causes in a single source of past experience negates the myriad of continuing influences on our lives including those which emanate

from the culture at large and, most importantly perhaps, those which concern our active intentions in the present".

Work with children in refuges in this country and elsewhere in the world has been of immense benefit to thousands of children and their mothers. Women working with children in Women's Aid have demonstrated commitment, understanding, energy, creativity and resourcefulness in this development to try to meet children's needs. The work could be of immense benefit to more children and to the wider community if it is well funded and supported, and continues to draw strength from its commitment to involving survivors of domestic violence in this work.

PART THREE

SUMMARY AND RECOMMENDATIONS

All the contributors describe what children have to say about their experience of domestic violence. What they say offers firm support to the evidence that children are deeply affected by witnessing domestic violence, whether or not they are themselves victims of the assaults. Children describe living with intolerable levels of fear, anxiety and stress which can cause them emotional, educational and developmental harm.

From the evidence presented there are unavoidable conclusions to be drawn about the needs of children in these circumstances. What follows is an account of our conclusions and some recommendations which emerge from them.

Many children living in violent households are physically abused themselves and likely to be at risk of abuse. In the ChildLine sample, 38 per cent of children had been assaulted. The association between domestic violence and child abuse has been increasingly well-documented (see Flitcraft and Evans; Farmer and Owens; Black) and drawn to public and professional attention by high profile cases, such as that of Sukina Hammond.

But this awareness does not seem to have permeated to child protection practice, as Farmer and Owen found in their recent research into child protection outcomes:

...in 59 per cent of the cases of children subject to physical abuse, neglect or emotional abuse there was concurrent violence in the family, usually inflicted by men to women. The associated risks and the fact that many of the children witnessed frequent violence to their mothers was given little attention by social workers. Yet domestic violence was a feature of most of the cases in the worst outcome groups."

Children who have not themselves been assaulted cannot be viewed as safe from harm. Indeed it is our contention - based on the evidence of children's calls to ChildLine - that many of these children suffer harm and some "significant harm" - the trigger for child protection under the Children Act 1989.

The notion of "significant harm" is laid down in the Children Act and discussed in subsequent government guidance. Carroll (Child Abuse Review, 1994) discusses the effect of the repeated trauma of domestic violence and the child's inability to fully recover from one episode before the next occurs. She refers to Bentovim's description of significant harm as:

"a compilation of significant events, both acute and long-standing, which interact with the child's ongoing development, and interrupt, alter, or impair physical and psychological development"

Carroll argues that "significant harm" involves *"avoidable damage occurring to a child which it is reasonable to expect parents to take steps to evade."* On these criteria, she argues that many children witnessing domestic violence are indeed suffering significant harm.

Yet there are major implications in proposing that these children should be more actively encompassed under sections 37 or 47 of the Children Act.

Section 47 outlines the duty of local authorities to investigate the circumstances of children about whom they, or are given cause to, consider may be at risk of suffering significant harm. Section 37 enables a court in family proceedings to require a local authority to investigate a child's circumstances to establish whether a care or supervision order should be made in cases of suspected harm to children.

Significant harm is not a clear, unproblematic concept. It is being more precisely defined by developing case law and there is growing debate among academics and practitioners about where the threshold lies and should lie.

In addition, there are growing concerns among child protection practitioners about the effectiveness of child protection procedures as a way of helping families where children are at risk. Many local authorities have unallocated child protection cases, and few are able to provide the essential prevention and therapeutic services alongside the increasing burden of child protection investigations. Resources are also becoming even tighter as the effects of the Government's Community Care policy begin to bite into departmental budgets.

On the one hand, there is agreement that children witnessing domestic violence do fall within the definition of significant harm would substantially aid greater recognition of their trauma and would move their needs further up the list of priorities. On the other hand, in practice, it is likely that they would continue to fall through the net.

In the current circumstances, it is also relevant to question whether an investigation which may result in the *child* being taken away from his or her mother, immediate friends and neighbourhood and placed in care is in the best interests of that child. Although the analysis of ChildLine's casenotes did show a few children (six) who asked to go into care, these were the exceptions. It was far more common for children to state categorically that they did not want to leave home or be separated from their family: they simply wanted the violence to stop. Some hoped that would be achieved by their fathers leaving; others by persuading their mothers to seek a divorce. There is a danger that children may be even more afraid of speaking out, if they fear the consequence will be removal from their home. Appropriate intervention is therefore vital.

Section 17 of the Children Act requires local authorities to provide family support services to children in need, covering many more children than those at risk of suffering significant harm. To date, however, establishing good non-stigmatic services appears to have taken second place to local authorities' child protection work. The Children Act Report 1993 commented: *"In general, progress towards full implementation of section 17 has been slow...some authorities are still finding it difficult to move from a reactive social policing role to a more proactive partnership role with families"* (para 2.39).

As it becomes increasingly clear that the child protection system only involves a small proportion of children and that there are many others who need support services, who currently fall outside the present system, the case for giving greater priority to preventative work through family support becomes more urgent. Working with the families, particularly the non-abusing parent (in most cases, the mother), may be far more beneficial to the child than a full investigative process, possibly resulting in that child's removal.

ChildLine, NISW and WAFE believe that a professional response to the needs of children witnessing domestic violence must be based on the views and desires of the child. Representation of the child's view on local domestic violence forums would also ensure that the needs of children are not overlooked by the many agencies seeking to formulate a common policy on domestic violence.

We believe that the recommendations below are a step towards setting a "child-led" policy for children involved in domestic violence.

Recommendations made jointly by ChildLine, Women's Aid Federation England and National Institute for Social Work

1.   Awareness of the effects of domestic violence on children and the links with child abuse

1.1   In order to help the child effectively, all agencies involved with children and parents must have an awareness of domestic violence, its effects on children and women and the links with child abuse.

1.2   Certain professionals have a specific role in relation to children experiencing domestic violence.   These include benefit, housing, police, educational and court welfare officers, social workers, health professionals and teachers.   We call upon them to develop appropriate policies to ensure that their practice does not undermine women's strategies to protect themselves and their children.

1.3   We have identified a particular need for awareness and training on these issues for social workers, health professionals, and for teachers and school staff.   These groups are most likely to have contact with children living with domestic violence.

2.   Social workers

2.1   Social workers are in a strong position to offer the practical and emotional support which abused women and their children need: this work should be seen in the context of the Audit Commission's report on preventative work.

2.2   There are important implications for the training of those who work in social services departments.   Both qualifying and in-service training should deal with the effects on children of witnessing domestic violence, and the associated risks for children.

2.3 Social workers should be more aware of the legislation related to domestic violence and inform women of their rights. In particular women should be informed about the power of the courts to oust the violent partner, to transfer the tenancy to the non-abusing parent and to exclude named individuals from the home.

2.4 The child's right to feel safe should not be over-ridden by the violent partner's desire for contact: if the child is reluctant to meet the father he or she should not be put under pressure to do so.

2.5 Clear distinctions need to be made and acknowledged between the abusing and non-abusing parent: good practice must support and empower women to protect themselves and their children.

2.6 Work in refuges should be recognised as an important area of social work: this includes making links with local refuges and setting up training for social workers.

3. Schools

3.1 Schools are often the child's first point of contact. Training needs to be available to both teaching and support staff on the issues relating to domestic violence.

3.2 Educational material for all children should be produced to give them a greater understanding of the realities of domestic violence. Children should be taught parenting skills as part of an overall commitment to teach children about alternatives to violent responses.

3.3 Schools need to liaise with their local Women's Aid group or refuge to ensure that the safety of women and children is not undermined, especially where there is a danger of the children being abducted. School staff should be aware of the dangers of disclosing the whereabouts of women and children escaping domestic violence.

4.   Health professionals

4.1   Domestic violence has damaging effects on the physical and mental health of children: male violence within the home is a serious public health issue for women and children. This means that training for all health professionals should include material on the recognition of violence and on appropriate responses. Relevant professionals include general practitioners, health visitors, paediatricians, community nurses and the nursing and medical staff of accident and emergency departments.

5.   Other professionals

5.1   All professionals who work with children should have training in awareness of domestic violence and its effects upon children.

6.   Supporting the child

6.1   Children affected by domestic violence need counselling and support. They need easy access to confidential services where they can talk about their experiences and discuss possible courses of action. We call for face-to-face counselling to be made available to these children, along with telephone counselling where appropriate.

6.2   Children experiencing domestic violence are clearly "children in need" as defined in section 17 of the Children Act. We call upon the Department of Health to issue a circular to social services departments, clarifying the status of children in leaving domestic violence as "children in need" under the Children Act 1989.

6.3   We believe that family support in the community, through family centres, Women's Aid groups, refuges and other community based initiatives, is a vital means of giving support to the mother and children. Local authorities should be recognise and support the development of services for children who experience domestic violence and work in partnership with other agencies and the voluntary sector to reach children in need.

6.4   All refuges should have a minimum of one full-time children's worker. There should be adequate staffing levels to meet the needs of women and children. Development of outreach and aftercare services for children should be supported.

6.5   Advocacy services for children experiencing domestic violence are urgently needed, so that children can make their voices heard when decisions are being made about their future.

6.6   Women's Aid provides a range of services for women and children, including emergency accommodation, advice, information, support and advocacy. A central funding strategy for refuge services should be put in place by government.

7.   Children's safety and the law

7.1   We endorse the following recommendations, made by the Law Commission in their report **Family Law: Domestic Violence and the Occupation of the Family Home**. The recommendations are concerned with legal measures which will strengthen the protection available to children from violence. The Lord Chancellor has already made a commitment to reviewing the law. At the time of publication the Family Homes and Domestic Violence Bill is before parliament.

7.2   Non molestation orders, or injunctions and occupation orders may be necessary to protect children. The Law Commission recommends that the need to secure the health, safety or well being of either the mother or any relevant child should be the court's primary consideration when deciding whether to grant such an order.

7.3   The Law Commission also recommends that the Children Act 1989 be amended to give the courts powers to make emergency ouster orders for the protection of children. The ouster order would exclude a named individual from the child's home, and could have a power of arrest attached to it.

7.4   The Children's Legal Centre recommends that children affected by domestic violence should be able to take independent legal action in the last resort, for example, to change their place of residence.

Section 9 of the Children Act allows children to seek a judge's permission to apply for a residence in their own right. We endorse this recommendation.

8.   Sharing Information

8.1   Inter-agency co-operation and sharing of information is a vital part of any professional response to domestic violence. We welcome the government's encouragement for the establishment of Inter-Agency Forums on domestic violence. All forums should include a representative from children's organisations, and where possible, a refuge children's worker, in order to properly ensure that the children's voices are not lost.

EPILOGUE

This publication grew out of my own personal experiences and so it feels appropriate that I should end on a personal note. In one form or another my father's violence has cast a long shadow over many people's lives. None is greater than the effects of my eldest brother's twelve-year estrangement from our mother. This has been the most painful legacy of male violence for our family.

I had always hoped that one day my mother would again share her life with her estranged son and his family. Tragically this will never happen. Our mother passed away unexpectedly in February this year.

Alex Saunders
1994

APPENDIX ONE

PERSONAL PROFILES OF PEOPLE INTERVIEWED
BY ALEX SAUNDERS

The names of my research participants have been changed, and personal details and the exact location of refuges omitted to ensure confidentiality.

Clara
Interviewed: 14 August 1992
Age: 19
Ethnic Origin: White European
In Refuge: 1979
Age on Arrival at Refuge: 5
Length of Stay: 9 months
Location: South London
Children's Worker: Part-time

John
Interviewed: 21 September 1992
Age: 27
Ethnic Origin: White European
In Refuge: 1978-1980
Age on Arrival at Refuge: 13
Length of Stay: 18 months
Location: South London
Children's Worker: Part-time

Sandra
Interviewed: 24 October 1992
Age: 23
Ethnic Origin: White European
In Refuge: 1978-1979
Age on Arrival at Refuge: 9
Length of Stay: 12 months
Location: Essex
Children's Worker: Part-time

Sophia
Interviewed: 25 October 1992
Age: 21
Ethnic Origin: White European
In Refuge: 1979-1980
Age on Arrival at Refuge: 8
Length of Stay: 14 months
Location: Essex
Children's Worker: Part-time

BIBLIOGRAPHY

Alessi, J. and Hearn, K. (1984) Group treatment of children in shelters for battered women, see Roberts, A.R. (ed.).

Association of Chief Officers of Probation (1992) *Association of Chief Officers of Probation Position Statement on Domestic Violence*, London: ACOP.

Ball, Mog (1990) *Children's Workers in Women's Aid Refuges: A Report on the Experience of Nine Refuges in England*, London: National Council of Voluntary Child Care Organisations.

Ball, M. (1990) *An Evaluation of the National Children's Worker Post and a Report on Children's Work in Seven Refuges funded by the BBC Children in Need Trust*, WAFE/Children in Need.

Ball, M. (1994) *Funding Refuge Services: A Study of Refuge Support Services for Women and Children Experiencing Domestic Violence*, Bristol: WAFE.

Barron, J. Harwin, N. and Singh, T. (1992) *Evidence to the Home Affairs Committee Enquiry into Domestic Violence*, Bristol: WAFE.

Bass, Ellen and Davies, Laura (1992) *The Courage to Heal: A Guide for Women Survivors of Child Sexual Abuse*, New York: HarperPerennial, A Division of HarperCollins Publishers, Inc. First published in 1988 by Harper & Row Publishers, Inc. Revised edition published in 1992.

Binney, Val, Harkell, Gina and Nixon, Judy (1981) *Leaving Violent Men: A Study of Refuges and Housing for Battered Women*, Leeds: Women's Aid Federation England.

Bogle, Marlene (1988) Brixton Black Women's Centre, *Feminist Review*, 28 (Spring).

Bowker, Lee, Arbitell, Michelle and McFerron, J. Richard (1988) On the relationship between wife beating and child abuse, in *Feminist Perspectives on Child Abuse*, Yllö, Kersti and Bograd, Michele (eds.) Beverly Hills, California: Sage Publications, Inc.

Bradshaw, J. (1990) *Child Poverty and Deprivation in the UK*, London: National Children's Bureau.

Bridge Child Care Consultancy Service (1991) *Sukina: An Evaluation Report of the Circumstances Leading to Her Death*, London: Bridge Child Care Consultancy Service.

Carlson, B. (1984) Children's observations of interpersonal violence, in *Battered Women and their Families*, Roberts, A.R. (ed.) New York: Springer.

Carroll, J. (1994) The protection of children exposed to marital violence, *Child Abuse Review*, Vol. 3, 6-14.

Charles, Nickie (1991) *Funding Women's Aid Services to the Community in Wales: Research Report*, Cardiff: Welsh Women's Aid, May 1991.

Children Act 1989, London: HMSO.

Children and Domestic Violence Interagency Group (1992) *Mission Statement: Philosophy of Intervention and Service Provision*, Port Lincoln (Southern Australia): Children and Domestic Violence Interagency Group.

Children in Parliament (1994) Issue 201, London: National Children's Bureau.

Christensen, L. (1990) Children's living conditions. An investigation into disregard of care in relation to children and teenagers in families of wife maltreatment, *Nordisk Psychologi*, Vol. 42, Mongraph No. 31, 161-232.

Clark, A. (1993) *Homeless Children and their Access to Schooling*, A Bristol Case Study, Bristol: SPACE Trust.

Department of Health (1990) *An Introduction to the Children Act 1989*, London: HMSO.

Department of Health (1994) *Children Act Report*, London: HMSO.

Dobash, Rebecca Emerson and Dobash, Russell, P. (1979) *Violence Against Wives: A Case Against the Patriarchy*, New York: The Free Press.

Dobash, Rebecca Emerson and Dobash, Russell, P. (1984) The nature and antecedents of violent events, *British Journal of Criminology*, 24 (3), 269-288.

Dobash, Rebecca Emerson and Dobash, Russell, P. (1992) *Women, Violence and Social Change*, London: Routledge.

Farmer, E. and Owen, M. (1993) *Decision-making, Intervention and Outcome in Child Protection Work*, Abstract of a report to the Department of Health, London: HMSO.

Forsstrom-Cohen, Barbara and Rosenbaum, Alan (1985) The effects of parental marital violence on young adults: an exploratory investigation, *Journal of Marriage and the Family*, 47 (2), 467-472.

Frankin, Bob (ed.) (1986) *The Rights of Children*, Oxford: Basil Blackwell Ltd.

Freeman, M.D.A. (1983) *The Rights and Wrongs of Children*, London: Frances Pinter.

Frost, Nick and Stein, Mike (1989) *The Politics of Child Welfare: inequality, Power and Change*, Hemel Hempstead: Harvester Wheatsheaf.

Garmezy, P. (1983) Stressors of childhood, in *Stress, Coping and Development in Children*, Garmezy, N. and Rutter, M. (eds.) New York: McGraw-Hill.

Gayford, J.J. (1975) Wife battering: a preliminary survey of 100 cases, *British Medical Journal*, 1 (January), 194-197.

Grusznski, Roger, Brink, James and Edleson, Jeffrey (1988) Support and education groups for children of battered women, *Child Welfare: Journal of Child Welfare League of America Inc.*, Vol. LXVII (5) (Sep/Oct), 431-444.

Hague, G. and Malos, E. (1993) *Domestic Violence: Action for Change*, Cheltenham: New Clarion Press.

Hendriks, Black and Caplan (1983) *When Father Kills Mother*, London: Routledge.

Hester, Marianne and Radford, Lorraine (1992) Domestic violence and access arrangements for children in Denmark and Britain, *Journal of Social Welfare and Family Law*, 1, 57-70.

Hoff, Lee Ann (1990) *Battered Women as Survivors*, London: Routledge.

Holden, G. and Ritchie, K. (1991) Linking extreme marital discord, child rearing and child behaviour problems: evidence from battered women, *Child Development*, 62 (2), (Apr), 311-327.

Hoyles, Martin (1989) *The Politics of Childhood*, illustrated by Phil Evans, London: Journeyman Press Ltd.

Hudson, Annie (1992) The child sexual abuse 'industry' and gender relations in social work, in *Women, Oppression and Social Work: Issues in Anti-Discriminatory Practice*, The State of Welfare series, Langan, Mary and Day, Lesley (eds.) London: Routledge.

Hughes, H. (1986) Research with children in shelters: implications for clinical services, *Children Today*, 21-25.

Jaffe, Peter, Wolfe, David and Wilson, Susan (1990) *Children of Battered Women*, Volume 21: Developmental Clinical Psychology and Psychiatry, Newbury Park, California: Sage Publications, Inc.

Kelly, L. (1994) The interconnectedness of domestic violence and child abuse: challenges for research, policy and practice, in Mullender and Morely (eds.) *Children Living with Domestic Violence: Putting Men's Abuse of Women on the Child Care Agenda*, pp 43-55, London: Whiting and Birch.

Law Commission (1992) *Family Law, Domestic Violence and Occupation of the Family Home*, Law Commission No. 207, London: HMSO.

Mama, Amina (1989) *The Hidden Struggle: Statutory and Voluntary Responses to Violence Against Black Women in the Home*, London: London Race and Housing Research Unit.

Maynard, M. (1985) The response of social workers to domestic violence, in *Private Violence and Public Policy: The Needs of Battered Women and the Response of the Public Services*, Pahl, Jan (ed.) London: Routledge and Kegan Paul.

McKinlay, Caroline and Singh, Thangam (1991) Giving peace a chance, *Child Care (Community Care Supplement)* (June) p5.

Mullender, A. and Morley, R. (1994) *Children Living with Domestic Violence: Putting Men's Abuse of Women on the Child Care Agenda*, London: Whiting and Birch.

National Council of Voluntary Child Care Organisations (n.d.) *Women's Aid and Child Care: Under Fives Initiative*, London: National Council of Voluntary Child Care Organisations.

O'Hara, Maureen (1990) Access visits that betray an abused child's trust, *Childright*, 70 (October), 17-18.

O'Hara, Maureen (1992) Domestic violence and child abuse - making the links, *Childright*, 88 (July), 4-5.

Pahl, J. (1995) Health professionals and violence against women, in *Family violence and the caring professions*, Kingston, P. and Penhale, B. (eds.), Milton Keynes: Open University.

Parton, Nigel (1990) Taking child abuse seriously, see Violence against Children Study Group (1990).

Parton, Christine (1990) Women, gender oppression and child abuse, see Violence against Children Study Group.

Pizzey, Erin (1974) *Scream Quietly or the Neighbours Will Hear*, Harmondsworth, Middlesex: Penguin Books Ltd.

Pizzey, Erin and Shapiro, Jeff (1982) *Prone to Violence*, London: Hamlyn Paperbacks.

Queensland Domestic Violence Task Force (1988) *Beyond These Walls*, Brisbane, Queensland: Report of the Queensland Domestic Violence Task Force.

Roberts, A.R. (ed.) (1984) *Battered Women and their Families*, New York: Springer.

Rosenberg, M. (1984) Inter-generational family violence: a critique and implications for witnessing children, paper presented at the 92nd annual convention of the American Psychological Association, Toronto. Cited in *Children of Battered Women*, see Jaffe, Peter, Wolfe, David and Wilson, Susan (1990).

Rutter, Michael and Madge, Nicola (1976) *Cycles of Disadvantage: A Review of Research*, London: Heinemann Educational Books Ltd.

Schechter, Susan (1982) *Women and Male Violence: The Visions and Struggles of the Battered Women's Movement*, London: Pluto Press.

Scottish Women's Aid (n.d.) *Working with Children in Women's Aid*, Dundee: Scottish Women's Aid.

Silvern, Louise and Kaersvang, Lynn (1989) The traumatized children of violent marriages, *Child Welfare: Journal of Child Welfare League of America, Inc*, Vol. LXVIII (4) (Jul/Aug), 421-436.

Smith, Lorna, (1989) *Domestic Violence: An Overview of the Literature*, Home Office Research Study No. 107, London: HMSO.

Stark, Evan and Flitcraft, Anne (1985) Woman-battering, child abuse and social heredity: what is the relationship? in *Marital Violence*, Johnson, Norman (ed.) Sociological Review Monograph 31, London: Routledge and Kegan Paul.

Stark, E. and Flitcraft, A. (1988) Women and children at risk: a feminist perspective on child abuse, *International Journal of Health Services*, 18, 1, pp 97-118.

Straus, Murray, Gelles, Richard and Steinmetz, Suzanne (1980) *Behind Closed Doors: Violence in the American Family*, New York: Anchor Books.

Suransky, Valerie (1982) *The Erosion of Childhood*, London: University of Chicago Press Ltd.

Victim Support (1992) *Domestic Violence: Report of a National Inter Agency Working Party on Domestic Violence*, London: Victim Support.

Violence against Children Study Group (1990) *Taking Child Abuse Seriously: Contemporary Issues in Child Protection Theory and Practice*, London: Unwin Hyman Ltd.

Walker, Lenore (1979) *The Battered Woman*, New York: Harper and Row, Publishers, Inc.

Wolfe, David, Jaffe, Peter, Wilson, Susan and Zak, L. (1985) Children of battered women: the relation of child behaviour to family violence and maternal stress, *Journal of Consulting and Clinical Psychology*, 53, 657-665.

Women's Aid Federation England (n.d.) *You can't Beat a Woman: Woman and Children in Refuges*, Bristol: Women's Aid Federation (England) Ltd.

Women's Aid Federation England (n.d.) *WAFE Statement of Aims and Principles*, Bristol: WAFE.

Women's Aid Federation England (1989) *Breaking Through: Women Surviving Male Violence*, Bristol: Women's Aid Federation (England) Ltd.

Women's Aid Federation England (1993) *Children's Rights Policy for Refuge Work*, Bristol: WAFE.

Yllö, K. and Bograd, M. (eds) (1988) *Feminist Perspectives on Wife Abuse*, Newbury Park, California: Sage.